I0622732

Dissertation

Mastery

Navigating Research, Writing, and Defense for Academic Success

by
Michael Missildine PhD

About the Author

Michael Missildine, PhD, hails from Amarillo, Texas, where he embarked on his illustrious law enforcement career, eventually leading him to his current role as an elected Justice of the Peace in Collin County. His journey through public service is marked by a notable 23-year tenure as a police officer, with significant roles including patrol supervisor and Chief Deputy.

As a Master Peace Officer, Dr. Missildine holds numerous certifications such as Basic Instructor, Firearms Instructor, Hostage Negotiator, and both Basic and Advanced SWAT. These credentials reflect his dedication and expertise in the field of law enforcement.

Academically, Dr. Missildine is equally accomplished. He possesses a Bachelor of Applied Arts and Sciences in Law Enforcement Administration, a Master of Public Administration, a Master of Science in Leadership, and a PhD in Organizational and Industrial Psychology. His extensive education underscores his deep understanding of law enforcement, public administration, and organizational dynamics.

In addition to his career in law enforcement and public service, Dr. Missildine serves as a commissioned officer in the Texas State Guard, holding a staff officer position in the headquarters unit of his Brigade. He is also a seasoned educator, having taught numerous classes to police officers, judges, and court staff, covering a wide range of topics from mental health to leadership.

On a personal note, Dr. Missildine is a family man, married with three adult sons and a grandson. His personal interests are as diverse as his professional achievements. He is passionate about writing, reading, and engaging in both PC and console gaming. A hands-on individual, he enjoys working on cars and trucks, as well as undertaking various projects around his house and yard.

Dr. Michael Missildine's multifaceted career and personal life highlight his commitment to public service, education, and family, making him a respected and admired figure in his community and beyond.

Table of Contents

Introduction:
Your Journey to Dissertation Mastery

When I was younger, I was fascinated with being a Doctor. At the time, I felt the journey was too long. An unobtainable goal that was out of reach. However, as I aged and became a little more wise to the world, I figured out that completing a dissertation is like any other major journey, you work on it one day and one step at a time. My dissertation chair said it perfectly, "It is a marathon, not a race." I took that statement to heart and focused on my journey little by little and step by step, eventually achieving my goal. You can reach your goal as well.

Welcome to the beginning of an adventure that's as challenging as it is rewarding. A journey where every step, from formulating a hypothesis to the final defense, is a critical piece of a puzzle that, when assembled, represents years of dedication, learning, and personal growth. This isn't just about obtaining a credential; it's about becoming a master of your chosen field, a specialist who contributes original thought to the world's collective knowledge. You are about to embark on your journey to dissertation mastery.

Think of this as a guidebook, a treasure map of sorts. It's here to lead you through the tangled jungle of academic research, past the pitfalls of writer's block, and over the mountainous terrain of data analysis. The path won't be smooth—there will be steep slopes and unexpected turns—but the strategies and insights contained in these pages aim to smooth some of the rougher patches and illuminate your path forward.

At the very foundation of your venture lies academic research. It's the bedrock upon which you will build your dissertation. Understanding this landscape is crucial—as is identifying a research question that sparks curiosity and drives discovery. And let's not forget the ethical considerations that serve as the moral compass for your voyage, ensuring that your research contributes positively to the great dialogue of academia.

A substantial component of your expedition will involve immersing yourself in a sea of literature. Navigating these waters requires more than a cursory glance at the surface. You'll need to dive deep, conducting thorough reviews while managing and organizing your findings in a way that supports your thesis and establishes your authority in the field.

Then comes the methodology—the blueprint of your study. This section is where many adventurers find themselves pausing, deliberating over the merits of qualitative versus quantitative methods, or wrestling with the finer points of their study design. Your decisions here will shape every aspect of your journey to come.

Data doesn't just sit there; it whispers secrets waiting to be heard. Through meticulous analysis, you'll discover patterns and narratives that, once interpreted, can change the course of your field or even spawn new avenues of inquiry. From fundamentals to software tools, you will learn to listen to the data and coax meaning from the numbers and themes you encounter.

But what good is discovery if it can't be shared? Academic writing—a craft in its own right—is the vessel for your voice. Structuring your dissertation and finding the scholarly tone can be an art form, one that demands practice and persistence. You'll learn to wield words like a seasoned smithy, shaping sentences into structures that can withstand the scrutiny of the most critical eyes.

No journeyman's work is beyond critique, and the peer review process is a trial by fire. Yet, much like steel forged in intense heat, your dissertation will emerge from this process stronger and more refined. Here, feedback isn't just about correction; it's a dialogue that pushes you to new heights of scholarly excellence.

As you near your destination, crafting a compelling discussion becomes paramount. You must link your results to your hypotheses, acknowledging the gaps while highlighting the significance of your work. And then, with nerves of steel, you will step into the spotlight to defend your findings, engaging with questions and critiques in real time.

But what happens once the confetti from your defense celebration has settled? Your work doesn't merely sit bound on a shelf; it reverberates through conference halls and journal pages, extending your impact far beyond the university walls. And as you ponder the roads yet to be traveled—be it academia, industry, or lifelong learning—you'll realize that this journey has equipped you with more than a title. It has prepared you for a future of inquiry, innovation, and inspiration.

This book embraces the complexity of the dissertation process without losing sight of its simplicity—a journey, much like life, is composed of steps. Some small and tentative, others bold and confident. Together, they lead you to mastery, not just of your dissertation but of the path you carve for yourself beyond it.

So, as you turn these pages, imagine them as the cobblestones beneath your feet. Each chapter, a stride forward. Each lesson learned, a mile gained. This is your path, laid out before you, ready for your first step. Whether you're a fresh-faced novice or have been on the trail for some time, this guidebook is here to accompany you to the culmination of your academic endeavor—your dissertation mastery.

With determination, adaptability, and this comprehensive guide at your side, the journey ahead won't merely lead to the attainment of a degree; it will signify your transformation into a scholar who stands ready to contribute meaningfully to the grand tapestry of human understanding and progress.

Let's set forth not just with the goal of finishing a task, but with the aim of mastering a craft. Along the way, let's embrace the struggles and triumphs, knowing that each challenge overcome is another element of expertise earned. Your journey to dissertation mastery starts now. Are you ready?

Chapter 1:
The Foundation of Academic Research

Embarking on the dissertation journey means finding your footing on the complex terrain of academic research, where the landscape stretches from the intricate details of your discipline to the towering norms of scholarly conduct. In navigating this terrain, it can't be overstated how crucial it is to first grasp the research landscape, where every study, like a single brushstroke, contributes to the larger picture of human knowledge (Booth, Colomb, & Williams, 2008). It's akin to understanding the lay of the land before plotting your expedition; you've got to know the current conversations, debates, and the unsolved puzzles of your field. However, it's not just about knowledge intake; identifying your own research question is about carving out a niche where your voice and contribution will not just echo but resonate (Clark & Creswell, 2014). Amid the excitement of these discoveries, you can't lose sight of the ethical compass that should guide every step you take; from respecting participant rights to navigating intellectual property, it's these principles that anchor our work in integrity and trust, ensuring that our scholarly contributions aren't just sound but also hold up to moral scrutiny (Resnik, 2011). Remember, laying a solid foundation in academic research is about more than just preparation; it's about crafting a launchpad for scholarly exploration that is as robust as it is responsible.

Understanding the Research Landscape is akin to mapping the terrain before setting out on a grand expedition. Just as a mountaineer needs to know the lay of the land, the challenges of the climb, and the potential paths to the summit, a doctoral candidate must understand the existing body of academic work, the complexities within their chosen field, and the unexplored questions that their research might address.

Embarking on a dissertation is no simple feat, and a savvy trailblazer knows that to chart a path, one must first survey the environment. What's been done? What discoveries primed the academic fields for your work? Where do gaps and opportunities lie? It's essential to grasp the scope of scholarly conversations and debates that precede your work—this is your foundation. Seek out major studies in your domain of interest because their insights and shortcomings can serve as stepping stones for your inquiry (Harzing & Alakangas, 2016).

Digging into previous research might seem like a monumental task, but it's a crucial and enlightening one. Think of it as attending a global symposium, where minds from all over the world have convened to wrestle with and explore ideas. You're not only learning here; you're scouting for allies, adversaries, and mentors in the guise of authors and their work (Boell & Cecez-Kecmanovic, 2015). You'll start to see patterns, debates, and perhaps most critically, the silences and spaces where your research can contribute.

The topography of the academic terrain is ever-changing, with new studies continually shaping and reshaping the landscape. Journals, conferences, and seminars are the shifting tectonics of this world, echoing the advancements and retreats of knowledge. To traverse this dynamic ground, you must keep abreast of developments: subscribe to relevant journals, join academic groups, attend conferences, and engage with the community they foster.

It's crucial to not just skim the surface but to delve into the historical strata of your field, understanding core theories and how they evolved. This historical insight helps you discern whether your research question is a product of contemporary trends or if it has deep, enduring roots (Suddaby, 2014). Sometimes, revisiting these scholarly artifacts reveals untapped veins for exploration or offers cautionary tales about exhausted mines.

Taking stock of methodology is a critical component of navigating the research landscape. In any given field, certain research methods will be more prevalent. Yet, even a dominant trend isn't a directive; it's an observation. For instance, if quantitative methods are the norm but qualitative methods can illuminate new aspects of a problem, you might have found your unique trailhead (Morse, 2016).

While exploring, also stay alert for interdisciplinary opportunities—perhaps the solutions to the puzzles in your field lie in borrowing tools or theories from another. Sometimes the freshest insights come from synthesizing information across disciplines, creating hybrid methodologies that can open up entirely new vistas of understanding (Repko, 2012).

Learning the language of the research landscape is like learning the local dialect of an unfamiliar region. Each discipline has its jargon, its shorthand, and its way of framing ideas. Proficiency in this language allows you to communicate effectively with other scholars, ensuring that your innovations resonate within the academic community.

It's also about identifying the current "hot spots"—areas where research is active and funding is flowing. While it may be tempting to head straight for these areas, remember: novelty can also be found in the less-traveled territories. Balancing your work between the cutting edge and the peripheral can yield substantial dividends.

Bear in mind, the research landscape isn't merely conceptual; it's sociopolitical. Power structures, funding bodies, and academia's own star system play roles in shaping which research gets noticed, nurtured, or neglected. Navigating this ecosystem intelligently requires understanding both the intellectual merit and the practical realities of your work (Willis, 2016).

Remember that the research landscape is not just external but internal as well. Reflect on your intellectual biases and assumptions. What part of the map are you naturally drawn to, and why? Understanding your own cognitive terrain is essential in identifying blind spots and achieving a balanced, critical perspective on the field you're about to contribute to.

In this digitally connected era, the research landscape extends far beyond the physical library. Digital databases, online forums, and social media platforms serve as both repositories of knowledge and arenas for scholarly discourse. Harnessing these resources effectively requires digital literacy and understanding the importance of digital engagement in disseminating and critiquing research.

Lastly, while understanding the research landscape, it's paramount to remain flexible and adaptable. Your initial conceptions of the field might evolve as you delve deeper, necessitating adjustments to your research plans. Remember, the strongest explorers are those willing to adjust their route when the landscape dictates a better course.

Taking all this into account as you map out your dissertation journey, you'll be better equipped to embark on a quest that's not only groundbreaking but also responsive to the contours and nuances of the academic world. The work of a doctoral candidate is to add meaningful contours to this already rich terrain, heightening its detail and contributing to its ever-evolving nature.

Identifying Your Research Question

Let's dive into the heart of your dissertation research: pinpointing that golden research question. In this quest for academic glory, nailing your research question is akin to hitting that sweet spot where curiosity meets contribution. The research question is your North Star, guiding you through the wilds of scholarship. The research question is the foundation to your dissertation. Picking the wrong question is like setting sail without a compass, so let's ensure you're chart-ready.

The best way to start is by asking yourself what lights a fire in your belly. What have you encountered in your field that's made you sit up and think, "Now there's a puzzle worth solving"? It's about straddling the line between the known and the great unknown. And remember, there's a fine line between a great research question and a wild goose chase.

So what's this elusive great research question look like? It's clear, focused, and, critically, answerable within the scope of your project (Booth, Colomb, & Williams, 2008). It should slice through the general noise and zero in on something specific. Think sniper, not shotgun. I can say that having been a SWAT operator for 5 years of my Law Enforcement career. And it's grounded in your research literature, which you'll get to grips with in chapter two, so it's not coming out of thin air but building on what's come before.

There are conventional, proven strategies for forming research questions -- detective work, essentially. Start by scouring the existing research for gaps or unanswered questions. Those gaps? They're potential gold mines for your inquiry. Think about contradictory findings or areas where the map says 'here be dragons.' That uncharted territory? That's your playground.

Consider your resources and limitations, too. If you're eyeing a question requiring a supercollider and a crack team of physicists, but you're a solo act with a laptop, you might want to recalibrate. Feasibility is the name of the game (Creswell & Creswell, 2017). Your research question needs to be tailored to what you can realistically manage given your context and constraints, as well as the rules or guidelines promulgated by your college or university.

As you orbit around potential topics, look for the intersection of relevance, interest, and originality. Does the question matter in the grand scheme of your field? Is it something that will keep you engaged during the long haul of a dissertation? More importantly, is it bringing something new to the table? The novelty is key, yet it must be balanced with practicality.

Also, be prepared to narrow it down. A broad question is a vast ocean that's tough to navigate and easy to drown in. It's fine to start wide but zoom in, layer by layer, until you've distilled your query to its essence. The more focused your question, the easier it will be to construct a clear and structured argument.

Reality check: your question won't survive in a vacuum. So, try to foresee how you might approach it methodologically. What data will you need? How will you collect it? Your question and the ways you can answer it are bound together – they should fit like a glove (Creswell & Creswell, 2017).

Envision the kind of study that could escort that research question to its answer. It's like planning a trip; pick the destination (your question) and then map out the route – what methods will you take, what tools do you need, who might you need to talk to along the way? This process demands creativity and a sprinkle of foresight.

Sometimes, the pressure to innovate can be overwhelming. But remember, not all research needs to reinvent the wheel. Often, it's the tiny tweaks or a new angle on an old problem that can bring the freshest insights. You're not trying to shatter the earth – just leave a dent that shows you were here.

As you refine your question, bounce ideas off your mentors and colleagues. They're your sounding board, and trust me, a fresh pair of eyes can save you from tunnel vision. They might ask, "So what?" And if your answer excites them, you're probably onto something. Feedback is gold; it can temper your ideas into something robust.

Document your thinking process – journal it, draw it, flowchart it, whatever works. There'll be evolution and, occasionally, revolution in your thinking. Keeping track lets you revisit and reflect on your journey – and sometimes, the seeds of the best ideas are buried in early scribbles.

To sum it up, identifying your research question is an intricate dance between what's been done, what could be done, and what you can do – wrapped up in the ribbon of your insatiable curiosity. It's the cornerstone of your dissertation, so give it the deliberation it deserves. With a well-crafted question in hand, you're not just embarking on a research project, you're setting forth on an adventure.

Ethics in Research

To weave some threads of ethical considerations into the rich tapestry of your dissertation journey, let's pivot to a critical, though sometimes less glamorous, aspect of academia: research ethics. Yep, that's the territory where the rubber meets the road, not just in doing your research right but in doing it responsibly.

Embarking on a research expedition isn't just about collecting data like seashells on the shoreline; it's also about respecting the environment where those shells are found. Ethical research encompasses far more than not fudging your numbers—though, let's be clear, that's pretty paramount. It's the pursuit of truth, the safeguarding of participants, and the context in which you're investigating your burning questions that all matter here.

First up, informed consent is a golden rule in the realm of research. Imagine you're inviting guests over—yes, your participants are your esteemed guests. You wouldn't just spring a surprise party on them; you'd tell them what to expect, the whys and the hows. That's informed consent: ensuring participants know what they're diving into and have freely agreed to participate (Fisher, 2013).

Now, confidentiality and anonymity are two peas in a pod in ethics-cuisine. It's about protecting the identities of those who graciously lend their experiences to your scholarly endeavors. Like a magician sworn to secrecy, you must ensure your participants' details don't accidentally show up in your final act (your dissertation).

When planning your research, also ponder over the potential risks and benefits. Make no mistake; it's not enough to scout the rewards your research may reap. Take a hard look at what could go wrong. Could your study inadvertently harm someone, physically or emotionally? Walk a mile in the shoes of your participants when evaluating these factors (Resnik, 2011).

Taking into account the population you're studying is also crucial. Vulnerable groups—the young, the elderly, individuals with cognitive impairments—demand extra layers of ethical consideration. Picture a mosaic, where pieces representing these groups need special settings to stay secure and intact within the larger picture of your research.

When it comes to data, integrity is the name of the game. Falsifying or cherry-picking data to suit a narrative isn't just frowned upon; it's a fast pass to Disasterville. As you collect and analyze your data, the ethos must be accuracy, and the path, transparency.

You've got to consider authorship ethics, too. If you're collaborating, ensure credit is given where it's due. Avoid ghostwriting scenarios and ensure all contributors can see the light of day in the byline of your work (Smith et al., 2019).

Also on the ticket is intellectual property respect. That means citing sources like there's no tomorrow because, in academia, your currency is references. Plagiarism is the heist of the intellectual world; don't let it sneak into your dissertation. Keep your sources attributed, your quotes in check, and know that there's grace in acknowledging the giants whose shoulders you stand on.

Moving along, consider the broader ethical implications of your research. What could be the societal impact of your findings? Are you pulling on threads that could unravel ethical dilemmas? Consider the ripples your scholarly pebble might make in the communal pond.

What about animal ethics, if your research crosses into non-human territories? The governing principle is the same: do no harm. Ensure you're adhering to the right guidelines and seeking out all the necessary approvals before proceeding (Animal Welfare Act, 1966).

Digging into the ethics of research also means being keenly aware of conflicts of interest. Whether it's financial, personal, or professional, these conflicts can skew your research's compass, diverting it away from the true north of objectivity. Declare and manage them like the potential hazards they are.

And hey, don't forget about the role of ethics committees and IRBs (Institutional Review Boards). These groups aren't there to rain on your research parade; they're more like the referees ensuring every play is fair. Engage with them early, understand their requirements, and respect their guidance—they're pivotal in the ethical orchestration of your research symphony.

As you document your procedures and findings, do it with ethical reporting in mind. Don't overstate your claims or underreport your errors. A balanced and honest account of your research is your contribution to the communal table of knowledge.

Lastly, remember that while your dissertation represents a significant milestone, it also pins your name to a piece of scholarly work forever. It's a legacy, in a way. One that you'll want to reflect integrity, thoroughness, and yes, ethics. Think of it as etching your name into the academia's hall of fame, with honour.

In sum, ethics in research isn't just a checkbox or a hurdle to clear; it's integrated into every step of your dissertation journey, from conception to conclusion. It's what elevates your work from being mere pages on a shelf to a well-respected and seminal piece of scholarship (Simons, 2015).

Chapter 3:
Literature Review Strategies

Carrying the torch from the foundational elements of academic research, Literature Review Strategies is your road map through the dense forest of scholarly publications. The chapter zeroes in on the essential tactics for scouting and corralling the vast array of sources you'll encounter. We'll nip in the bud the tendency to merely accumulate articles and instead, foster a strategy for conducting a meticulous and comprehensive review. Here, we're talking about the art of sieving through heaps of data to uncover the golden nuggets that are deeply relevant to your research question. It's like panning for gold in a river swarming with possibilities – you've got to know where to look and how to recognize the real deal. As you may guess, digesting and intertwining these literary pieces is no less than crafting a fine tapestry, and this chapter will guide you with the finesse required to synthesize your findings, developing a narrative that's both coherent and compelling. To top it off, we'll delve into the nuts and bolts of managing the behemoth that your literature collection threatens to become, ensuring that you're organizing and archiving like a pro, so not a single invaluable reference goes missing when it's showtime (Randolph, 2009; Hart, 2018). Your literature review will be comprised of more than 20 pages of your dissertation, so it will be the largest part of the entire document. The premise here is simple: it's not just about what you know; it's about how you harness that knowledge effectively within your academic endeavor.

Conducting a Comprehensive Review is like donning a detective's hat and embarking on an elusive quest for clues. This endeavor, my friends, is not merely about gathering a stack of relevant articles; it's about piercing together an intellectual tapestry that paints a comprehensive backdrop for your dissertation. Certainly, it'll be a painstaking journey, but it's one where diligence pays off in the form of rich insights and robust arguments.

Let's start with the cornerstone of your review: identifying your sources. This isn't just about spotting a few high-profile studies and calling it a day. It requires you to dig deep into databases, sift through scholarly journals, and maybe even cozy up to some dust-covered tomes in the very depths of your university library. Your goal here is meticulous inclusivity, ensuring you cover not only the seminal works but also the lesser-known studies that could provide unique nuances to your research (Booth, Colomb, & Williams, 2008).

Now, you might wonder, what's the scope of comprehensive? It will vary, of course, according to the breathlessness of your topic. High-level articles and books will give you broad strokes, but you'd be amiss if you overlooked the importance of those technical reports, conference proceedings, and even dissertations that came before yours. Indeed, some of the most valuable pearls of wisdom may be nestled in the footnotes and bibliographies of other research papers (Hart, 1998).

As you're plunging into this sea of literature, you must not drown in irrelevance. Establish clear inclusion and exclusion criteria for your sources. What's the time frame you're looking at? Are there particular methodologies or populations you're focusing on? By setting these parameters, you wave off that overwhelming surge of data that doesn't quite align with your research question (Randolph, 2009).

Your collection of academic papers is starting to look quite majestic, but it's not time to ease up on the throttle just yet. A keystone of conducting a comprehensive review is staying on top of the literature. You see, research is a dynamic beast, and what was groundbreaking a month ago might already be on its way to obsolesce today. Set alerts for key journals, subscribe to updates in your area of study, and keep tabs on those leading-edge researchers whose work could be pivotally linked to yours.

A diverse set of perspectives is crucial. It's easy to become ensconced in research that resonates with your own perspectives, so actively seek out studies that challenge or differ from your views. This isn't about intellectual masochism; it's about ensuring that your review is as comprehensive and balanced as possible, which ultimately strengthens the credibility and depth of your dissertation.

There's a fable in the academic world suggesting that one must read every paper word for word. Let's dispel that myth now. You need a strategy to efficiently sift through the tidal wave of information. Start with abstracts to discern relevance, then perhaps move to conclusions or discussions to assess the weight and implications for your study. Full reads are reserved for those seminal works that are most critical to your thesis (Booth et al., 2008).

Don't just ingest this literature – engage with it. Annotate articles, jot down ideas as they come, and discuss findings with peers or mentors. This is not merely passive reading; this is active academic digestion. You're fueling the engine of synthesis that will drive the next phase of your research journey.

Throughout this process, you're building a foundation, but be wary of confirmation bias, that sneaky saboteur. You're not looking merely for evidence that supports your hypotheses; you're combing for the truth, wherever that may lead. Counterarguments and alternative explanations are not threats; they're the pressure that forms the diamonds of insight in your work.

Organize as you go. A comprehensive review is as good as the structure that supports it. Categorize your findings thematically, methodologically, or chronologically – whichever serves your dissertation best. This will save you a Herculean effort later as you synthesize and craft your narrative (Hart, 1998).

Remember, as you dive into this ocean of knowledge, that your review isn't just about what's known – it's equally about identifying gaps. Where is the silence deafening? What questions remain unanswered? It is within these voids that your study will find its voice and contribute something new to the academic chorus.

Amid all this, quality trumps quantity. The number of sources is not a badge of honor; their relevance and impact are what truly matters. It's about mapping the contours of the existing landscape to determine where you can build your innovative edifice of research.

Don't forget the golden rule of comprehensive reviews: citation, citation, citation. Each idea that isn't wholly your own should be attributed to its originator meticulously and consistently, following the academic standards of your field, such as APA style (American Psychological Association, 2020). Anything less is academic heresy.

As this journey of exploration winds down, and you find yourself armed with a wealth of information, don't be surprised if your initial research questions evolve. With this newfound understanding comes the flexibility to refine your focus, ensuring that your dissertation is not just a mirror of what's known, but a beacon for what's next.

Finally, understand that conducting a comprehensive review is an iterative process. It's akin to painting a masterpiece; initial strokes are seldom the final ones. Return to the literature often; reflect, refine, and reanalyze as you progress. Your review is not just a chapter of your dissertation – it's a continuously unfolding narrative that supports everything that follows.

Shoulders might tense at the weight of such an endeavor, but remember that this comprehensive review is the bedrock upon which your entire dissertation stands. Treat it with the respect it demands, and it will not only illuminate your path but also enlighten others who tread the academic trails behind you. Now go forth, sift, discern, and weave the scholarly threads that will form the vibrant tapestry of your research success.

Synthesizing Sources

You've collected an impressive stack of journal articles, books, reports, and other scholarly materials. The challenge now is not just to read these sources but to weave them together into a coherent narrative that supports your research. This is, essentially, your opportunity to let all these various characters at the intellectual party you've been inviting to converse, debate, and perhaps even disagree. And, let me tell you, synchronizing these voices isn't a walk in the academic park.

Synthesizing sources is like orchestrating a complex musical arrangement. Each source is an instrument, bringing its own timbre to the melody. Your task is to ensure that they play in harmony, creating a sound that is richer than its parts (Boote & Beile, 2005). The synthesis goes beyond summarising; it requires interpretation and a clear understanding of how each piece contributes to the overall theme of your research.

Think of it this way: you're at the helm of a ship filled with ideas. Some might rush ahead, full of energy and new perspectives, while others act like anchors, grounding your research in established theory. Your job is to navigate these waters, steering away from redundant information while highlighting revolutionary thoughts that push your discipline's boundaries.

Start with thematic grouping. Cluster your sources by the themes, issues, or concepts they discuss (Boote & Beile, 2005). This isn't about organizing your library by color or size but by the intrinsic ideas they contribute. Patterns will begin to emerge—trends that traverse multiple writings and gaps as noticeable as the silence in a paused symphony.

As you cluster, you'll identify the landmark studies—the big hitters. These are the pivotal works that have shaped the discourse within your field. They're often cited by multiple other sources and are invaluable in providing historical context and a benchmark for your own work (Webster & Watson, 2002).

Now, let's talk contrapuntal reading. In music, counterpoint is the art of combining distinct melodic lines into a single harmonic texture. Similarly, read your sources against each other, noting where they collaborate or contradict. It's not enough to know what Smith says about urban sustainability; you've got to know how that resonates or clashes with what Osei has mentioned on a similar subject. These points of agreement or contention are the sweet spots where synthesis thrives.

A common trap is to fall into what's called 'list-like writing.' That's where you end up merely cataloging what each source says about a topic. Fight this urge. You're not creating a 'who-said-what' list; you're drawing larger conclusions and showing how one idea flows into another to support your thesis.

Take advantage of tables and concept maps to visualize relationships and interactions among sources. A table can compare and contrast theories, methodologies, or findings. A concept map can help you see how one author's ideas branch out, interweave with others, form patterns, or identify a void like a black hole of unsolved mysteries waiting for your daring venture (Webster & Watson, 2002).

When synthesizing, remember to approach each source critically. Don't take findings at face value; consider the research methodology, the sample size, the context, and the conclusions drawn. Ask yourself why this source has chosen these methods, this path—and how it relates to your work.

Don't forget the synthesis happens within paragraphs too. You're not writing a shopping list where everything is given space in a linear, predictable fashion. You're more like a chef, skillfully layering flavors. A pinch of Jones' theoretical framework, a spoonful of Patel's empirical findings, and a dash of Nguyen's critical perspective.

Throughout your paragraphs, blend and bind these ideas, making strong connections and transitions that form a seamless narrative (Boote & Beile, 2005).

And as you synthesize, keep your research question in the limelight. It's the gravitational center that holds this expanding universe of thoughts together. Each connection you draw between sources, each insight you draw from them, should propel your research question forward.

Finally, I can't stress enough the importance of maintaining your scholarly voice throughout this process. This symphony is yours, and while the instruments have come from others, the tune they play is uniquely defined by your direction, your perspective. Make it clear when you are presenting others' thoughts vs. when you're drawing your own conclusions.

By blending these many voices into a cohesive and insightful narrative, you will position yourself as a thoughtful scholar ready to contribute a meaningful verse to the ongoing academic conversation. Stay flexible, stay curious, and let the synthesis reveal its own story as you go.

Summarily, synthesizing sources is the crux of a literature review. It's your chance to make sense of the dialogue in your field, and it's where you begin to lay the groundwork for your novel contribution to knowledge. Remember, synthesis is not a process of selecting and summarizing but rather one of critical thinking and intellectual choreography.

Managing and Organizing Literature Let's dive into the nitty-gritty of managing and organizing literature, shall we? As you've been plundering through texts, articles, and all manner of scholarly documents, it's paramount to have a system that keeps you from drowning in a sea of information. After all, a dissertation is a hefty project, and without some semblance of order, you're setting yourself up for a wild labyrinthine adventure – minus the excitement.

First things first, you'll need a literature management tool. There's a slew of software options out there designed to make your life easier. Programs like Zotero, Mendeley, or EndNote can help you gather, manage, and cite research material with a few clicks and keystrokes (Franzosi, 2016). These tools provide a searchable database of your literature, which is like having your own personal library catalog without the 'ssshh-ing' librarian.

Once you've selected a tool that jives with your vibe, it's time to get your digital library populated. Enter each source diligently, making sure all the relevant details (author, year, title, publication, etc.) are correctly entered. Misplaced or missing information can be a real pain later on, trust me.

Here's a trick – as you add literature to your database, tag it with keywords relating to your research question and themes. This will make it a breeze to filter and find the resources you need when it's time to write. You could be looking for every paper ever written on 'narrative therapy in the wild,' and with a couple of tags, they're at your fingertips (Bramer, Rethlefsen, Kleijnen, & Franco, 2017).

And don't just stop with abstracts. Full-text PDFs can usually be attached directly to your database entries. This saves you from the future headache of having to scramble through various folders on your laptop or thumbing through physical copies trying to locate that one crucial piece you remember skimming over at 2 a.m. during a research rampage.

Let's talk notes. As you're reading, take insightful notes directly in your literature management tool or in a separate, linked digital notebook. It's like leaving breadcrumbs for yourself so that you can easily backtrack to significant thoughts and quotes without rerunning the whole trail.

After you've flung yourself far and wide across the extensiveness of your topic, a synthesis matrix can help you draw connections between your sources. It's a simple yet powerful spreadsheet where you break down the common themes, methodologies, findings, and gaps in the literature. Think of it as the bones of your literature review, where every row aligns to a source while columns signify the elements you're comparing across all literature (Onwuegbuzie & Frels, 2016).

Remember, consistency in your approach to managing literature will pay dividends. Set aside time regularly to update your database and keep your matrix polished—that way, you're not cramming it all in right before a meeting with your advisor. Such cram sessions can make you feel like you're trying to prepare a five-course meal in a microwave.

Speaking of advisors, they're like the ace up your sleeve. Share your organizational tools with them so they can help guide you on which sources are pure gold and which ones are just fool's gold. Collaboration tools within your literature management system can enable this smoothly.

Categorization is a godsend. When organizing literature, consider labeling entries by relevance or by stages in your dissertation. For example, sources relevant to your methodology could be in one category, while those supporting your literature review's themes could be in another. Suddenly, what seemed like an insurmountable mountain of reading material becomes a series of small, climbable hills.

Don't forget about backing up. All this organization would mean zilch if your computer decides to take an unexpected siesta, along with all your work. Regular backups to the cloud or an external hard drive will ensure that even in the face of technical adversity, your literature collection remains intact.

Lastly, periodic reviews of your literature management system are as crucial as the initial organization. As your research evolves, you might find certain themes become more or less important, or new research may emerge. Revisit and revise your database, notes, and synthesis matrix to reflect these changes and stay current.

With these strategies in your toolkit, managing and organizing literature should feel less like a chaotic whirlwind and more like a deliberate, albeit complex, dance. You're not just throwing papers into a pile; you're curating a library, a base camp for your ascension to the academic summit.

Now, let's not kid ourselves – managing and organizing literature is a task that can sometimes feel as endless as the sky itself. But it's a task that, when done with care and consideration, makes the rest of the journey smoother and the final destination that much clearer.

And there you have it, the method behind the madness of managing and organizing literature. As you're sorting through stacks of articles and books, embracing the disorderly order of discovery, keep in mind that every note you take, every source you catalog, is laying another stone on the path to your academic masterpiece.

Chapter 3:
Methodology Mastery

Building on the solid foundation of academic research and the rich tapestry of your literature review, it's time to roll up your sleeves and carve out the heart of your dissertation—your methodology. Think of this chapter as the engine room of your research vessel, where you'll decide whether to navigate the waters of qualitative inquiry, with its rich, narrative-driven insights, or steer toward the charts of quantitative analysis, with its numerical rigor and statistical finesse. But it's not just about picking tools; it's about crafting that perfect blend of science and storytelling that suits your question to a T. You're the architect here, skillfully designing your study, blueprinting data collection to precision while ensuring reliability and validity aren't lost in the shuffle (Creswell & Creswell, 2017). The methodology isn't just a section; it's a pledge of transparency for your peers and a promise of integrity to your field—a meticulous mold from which your findings will emerge, sculpted with care, to stand the test of scrutiny and secure your place in the annals of academic excellence (Bryman, 2016).

Qualitative vs. Quantitative Methods

When you dive deep into the world of dissertation methodologies, you're bound to encounter the long-standing debate of qualitative versus quantitative methods. It's like choosing between a paintbrush and a ruler: both tools, vastly different, but essential depending on the masterpiece you're crafting. This section aims to unravel the complexities, strengths, and when to use each approach. It's not just picking sides; it's about aligning your research question with the most effective method to interrogate it. My dissertation utilized quantitative methodology as I was more interested in the mathematics of research instead of the lived experience with qualitative methodologies.

Let's kick things off with quantitative methods, which are akin to the building blocks of scientific research. They're all about numbers, objective measurements, and statistical analysis. Think of quantitative research as a matter of 'how many' or 'how much.' It can offer insights through surveys, experiments, and numerical data. For instance, if you're investigating the prevalence of a particular phenomenon, quantitative data can give you an exact count or percentage that qualifies your findings and offers a level of generalizability (Creswell, 2014).

Quantitative research also shines when it comes to its predictive power. Because it's rooted in mathematical rigor, the findings derived from this approach aren't just flukes but patterns and relationships that withstand the test of statistical scrutiny. You're playing the role of a detective, looking for clues that tell a coherent story based on empirical evidence. What's more, it's often seen as more 'scientific', winning brownie points from certain scholarly circles that still regard numbers as the epitome of objectivity.

Flipping the script, qualitative methods provide a different flavor to your research palate. They're about understanding the 'why' and 'how' behind human behavior. If quantitative is the skeleton, qualitative is the flesh and blood, providing context, depth, and color to the bare bones of numbers. It involves interviews, observations, and text analysis, aiming to extract themes and patterns through an interpretive lens (Merriam & Tisdell, 2015).

By employing qualitative methods, you become an explorer, mapping the rich, often uncharted territories of human experience. It's particularly powerful when dealing with complex phenomena that can't be reduced to mere numbers. At its best, qualitative research tells a story, offering a window into the subjective worlds of your participants. It's about immersion, understanding context, culture, and the myriad factors that shape human behavior.

But here's the twist: these methods aren't mutually exclusive. They're more complementary than you might think. Entering the realm of mixed methods, you can harness the strengths of both. Imagine being able to measure the extent of a phenomenon with quantitative accuracy, then peel back the layers to explore the human nuances behind those numbers qualitatively.

Balancing the two, choosing the optimal research journey requires a deep understanding of your research problem. What are you really after? Is it the statistical weight of widespread trends or the rich, detailed descriptions of personal experiences? A well-curated research design marries your question with the right approach to yield convincing, impactful findings.

Now, let's factor in reliability and validity. For quantitative research, you're aiming for results that others can replicate and verify, instilling a sense of confidence in the reliability of your measurements (Shuttleworth, 2008). Validation here means ensuring your results accurately reflect what you're trying to measure. That your survey, for example, truly captures the attitudes or behaviors in question.

Qualitative work, in contrast, can be trickier to replicate given its subjectivity. Yet, its validity isn't any less vital. It's about proving your interpretation fits the data, that your explanation makes sense within the context you've studied. Establishing trustworthiness in qualitative studies involves credibility, transferability, dependability, and confirmability. You're showing that if someone else followed your path, they'd understand how you reached your conclusions.

So, as you sit down to blueprint your dissertation, let's not get pigeonholed into thinking one method is inherently superior to the other. Both quantitative and qualitative methods have their place on the lofty shelves of academic rigor. They simply serve different ends. Your task as a burgeoning scholar is to articulate a clear rationale for your chosen method, ensuring it aligns with your objectives and research questions.

Choosing between qualitative and quantitative methods also sets the tone for the rest of your dissertation journey. With quantitative research, you're equipping yourself for the statistical battleground, sharpening your SPSS or R skills to tame the beast of data into submission. Qualitative research, on the other hand, may find you deciphering transcripts, weaving through narratives to unearth the subtleties and intricacies of human thought and behavior.

Let's not forget the audiences you're addressing. Certain disciplines may lean heavily towards one method over the other. For instance, psychology has a strong quantitative tradition, whereas anthropology luxuriates in qualitative depths. Knowing the predilections of your field can guide not only your methodology but also how you present and defend your work to your dissertation committee members.

Let me underscore that at the heart of the choice between qualitative and quantitative methods is your purpose. What's the essence of what you're trying to uncover? If it can be counted, measured, and statistically analyzed, then head on down the quantitative road. If it's about capturing experiences, perceptions, and the richness of human life, then qualitative may be your best bet. But always, the golden rule is alignment: between your questions, your methods, and your goals.

As you gear up to venture into the exciting landscape of your research, embrace the diversity of approaches at your disposal. Whether you skew towards the data-driven precision of quantitative methods or the narrative-rich explorations of qualitative ones, you can craft a compelling dissertation narrative. And remember, combining the two through mixed methods can yield a robust, multi-faceted understanding of your research question.

Designing Your Study

Diving headfirst into your dissertational waters, you need to have a blueprint that will navigate you through tumultuous waves and lead you to the shore of successful completion. Designing your study is akin to drafting architectural plans before raising a building—it's all about ensuring that your research has the structure and precision required for rigorous investigation. Also, try not to re-invent the wheel. Look for a study that may allow for a continuation study.

Firstly, let's talk about the research design. What's that, you ask? Simply put, it's the backbone of your study—the strategy that outlines what you'll investigate, the means you'll employ, and how you'll interpret your findings (Yin, 2018). It encompasses your research question, hypothesis (if any), data collection and analysis methods, and ultimately steers the direction of your scholarly work.

Selecting a suitable design starts with a clear understanding of your research objectives. Are you attempting to explore a phenomenon? Then qualitative routes, with their narrative richness, may be up your alley. But if you're after the 'what' and 'how much'—quantitative measures are your ticket to scores of data ready to be quantified (Creswell & Creswell, 2017).

Now, don't get caught in the binary trap. Mixed methods designs blend both qualitative and quantitative approaches to give you a comprehensive view of your research puzzle. The synergy of combining both types can provide you with a more complex and complete understanding (Morse, 1991). Most universities discourage students from attempting a mixed method approach for the first dissertation as it is much more in depth and requires more work than a singular quantitative or qualitative methodology.

Let's push forward—it's time to think about your study's scope. A common snag here is biting off more than you can chew. Be realistic about the sample size and the extent of data you can manage. Remember, the key isn't always to aim for grandeur but rather accuracy and manageability.

The reliability and validity of your study are the bedrock ensuring that what you're measuring is indeed what you set out to measure. These concepts can intimidate, but don't let them spook you. They're essentially safeguards that ensure your study can be trusted and its findings applicable (Heale & Twycross, 2015).

Another piece of the design puzzle is your methodology's ethical considerations. This is no afterthought; ethical protocols are central to your study's integrity. Anonymity, informed consent, and confidentiality are pillars you can't afford to skim over.

Let's touch on operational definitions. When you specify the terms and variables, your study stands on a firm ground where ambiguity is shown the door. If you say 'social media engagement', you better have a clear definition that the reader can understand and replicate.

Data collection is your next frontier. Whether you're surveying, interviewing, or observing, each method must be well-calibrated to your study's needs. And let's not overlook the tools you'll use—a wrongly chosen survey platform or a misaligned analytic software can send you back several steps.

Sampling strategies are another crux of your design. Whether random, stratified, or purposive, your sampling method should align with your goals and ensure fair representation (Etikan, Musa, & Alkassim, 2016). No one wants a skewed study that reflects just a tiny niche unless, of course, that's your explicit aim.

What about the dreaded limitations? Face them head-on by acknowledging potential weaknesses in your design upfront. This not only exhibits scholarly integrity but also brackets your readers' expectations.

As your design converges, a timeline becomes your steering wheel. Keeping your study within realistic temporal boundaries prevents burnout and maintains momentum.

Lastly, piloting your study can be a stethoscope for your research's heartbeat. Running a small-scale version can reveal pitfalls before you're too deep in, saving you the heartache of glaring oversights.

Overall, designing your study is a balance of science and creativity. It demands careful consideration but also leaves room for innovation. Craft your study design wisely, and it will speak volumes of your work before a single word of your findings is written.

In conclusion, the study's design dictates its flow and impact. Your role is to craft it with precision, practicality, and foresight. A well-designed study is the first step toward standing on the stage of academic recognition, your dissertation held triumphantly in hand.

Data Collection Techniques

Let's talk about diving into the trenches of your research, where the rubber meets the road: collecting your data. Data collection is like a detective's investigation—it's the gritty, sometimes messy foray into the world of facts, figures, and narratives that will shape your dissertation. Now, we should clarify that 'techniques' isn't just about the tools you wield; it's also about the strategy, the timing, and the precision with which you employ these tools to gather information.

First up, you've got surveys and questionnaires, classic instruments that are like swiss army knives for the quantitative researcher. Crafting these requires a knack for clarity and an anticipation of how people think and feel. It's not just about asking the right questions; it's about asking questions right. The way you phrase a question can be the difference between a data goldmine and a statistical nightmare (Sue & Ritter, 2012).

Let's not forget interviews. If surveys are the sniper rifles of data collection, interviews are the shotguns—broad, impactful, and rich in detail. Whether structured or free-flowing, they reveal nuances in participant responses that numbers alone can't capture. Practicing the art of listening in interviews is like jazz; it's a delicate dance of give and take, weaving through the melodies of human experience (DiCicco-Bloom & Crabtree, 2006).

Then there's the art of observation, where you become a fly on the wall, watching and recording the world in its natural state. This technique requires a stealthy blend of invisibility and attentiveness. It's as much about what you see as what you don't. As an observer, you're capturing the raw materials that can either reinforce or dismantle the polished narratives we often tell ourselves (Angrosino & Rosenberg, 2011).

With advancements in technology, data collection has also gone digital. Online tools and mobile apps are now part of the researcher's arsenal, serving as extensions of our senses. From web analytics to social media trends, virtual footprints are as telling as their physical counterparts. In the cyber realm, data often flows like a torrent; the skill lies in building the dams and channels to capture it effectively (Boyd & Crawford, 2012).

A lesser-discussed but vital technique is document analysis. It's the historian's spoon, slowly but surely excavating layers of the past through archives, records, and reports. Document analysis requires a discerning eye to distinguish between what is said and what is meant, to read between the lines of text and find the truths hidden within (Prior, 2003).

What's crucial in all these techniques is the concept of sampling. You don't need to interrogate every grain of sand on the beach to know it's a beach. Proper sampling can give you a reliable representation of the larger population. It's about balance—too narrow a sample and you risk missing the landscape; too broad, and you're wading through unnecessary detail. Crafting that perfect sample is a bit like alchemy—part science, part intuition (Thompson, 2012).

Now, remember, just picking a method isn't enough; you must also consider validity and reliability. It's like tuning a guitar; your data collection method needs to sound true note after note, time after time. Ensure that your technique accurately measures what it's supposed to and that repeating the process would yield the same results under consistent conditions (Golafshani, 2003).

It's all about the ethical protocol, too. Data collection isn't a free-for-all; it's a careful step-by-step process where respect for participants' rights and confidentiality is paramount. Treat your subjects' information like a sacred trust, because that's exactly what it is. Ethical mishaps can turn a dissertation dream into an academic nightmare (Resnik, 2011).

For qualitative aficionados, don't overlook case studies. They're like mini-universes, rich with complexity, revealing the layers and textures of a single instance that resonate with universal truths. Building a case study is akin to crafting a novel; it's storytelling with a purpose, grounded in real-world evidence (Yin, 2013).

And let's not forget the power of longitudinal studies—tracking data over time to catch the ebb and flow of trends. It's like setting up a time-lapse camera on your subject, revealing transformations that other techniques might miss. The decisiveness of longitudinal data can underscore your findings with the weight of temporality (Menard, 2002).

Of course, no data collection technique is an island. Triangulation—using multiple methods or sources to cross-verify your findings—can turn a shaky hypothesis into concrete conclusions. It's like forming a rock band; where one instrument falters, the others pick up the slack, creating a harmony of evidence that's hard to dispute (Denzin, 1978).

And remember, while you're out there collecting data, stay flexible. Sometimes the most well-planned data collection expedition encounters the unexpected. Think of it as jazz improvisation; take those surprises and riff on them, because they just might lead to the most profound insights of your research.

In closing, your data collection journey should be approached with care, creativity, and a healthy respect for the rich, messy, and wonderous world of research. Whether you're surveying from the high-rise or interviewing in the trenches, remember that these data points are more than just numbers or words; they are the brushstrokes that will paint the canvas of your dissertation.

So, there you have it. A myriad of techniques awaits your command. Choose wisely, execute deftly, and your data will sing the truths you seek to uncover. Your dissertation isn't just a document; it's a testament to your journey as a researcher. Treat every data point like a clue, and the story you unravel will be one worth telling.

Chapter 4:
The Art of Analyzing Data

Diving headfirst into the world of data can feel like deciphering an enigmatic code from another dimension, but fear not, for this chapter is your cipher. We're about to embark on a journey through the art of analyzing data, where you'll learn not just to make sense of the figures before you, but to weave them into a compelling narrative that underpins your research findings. Imagine you're cracking open a chest of untold treasures, each data point a glinting gem that, when correctly appraised, adds value to the wealth of your scholarly work. Here's where your research design from Chapter 3 transforms into actionable insights, through meticulous dissection and interpretation. It's essential to understand there's a rhythm to it—balancing between the statistical precision of quantitative data and the nuanced interpretations of qualitative insights. It's not about mistrusting your gut, but rather, marrying intuition with the rigidity of scientific method; ground your hunches in the hard evidence. As you shuffle through mountains of data, remember that each piece plays a pivotal role in painting the bigger picture (Creswell & Creswell, 2017). Of course, you'll be in good company with software tools which can help automate and refine this process, but be wary not to let them override the human touch—it's your analysis that makes the narrative dance. Overall, through mastering the techniques of effective data analysis, you'll not only sharpen your argument but also set a solid stage for the critique and discussions that will follow (Maxwell, 2012).

Data Analysis Fundamentals

As we delve into the heart of your dissertation's empirical world, familiarizing yourself with data analysis fundamentals is akin to a chef understanding their ingredients—it's crucial to the success of the final dish. In this context, your 'dish' is a robust, compelling, and believable set of conclusions drawn from your carefully collected data. Now, what exactly are these fundamentals, and why are they so vital?

First off, let's clear the air: analyzing data isn't about complex statistical equations (exclusively, at least) or showing off how many analytical acronyms you can fit into one sentence. It's about making sense, telling a story, and, most importantly, supporting that narrative with strong, unambiguous evidence. To achieve this, we'll start with the basics—understanding the types of data at your disposal.

Quantitative data, or numbers, and qualitative data, or words, require different analytical treatments. Quantitative analysis may involve statistical tests that lend themselves to numerical computation, like regressions or factor analysis (Creswell & Creswell, 2017). On the flip side, qualitative analysis often involves coding, themes emergence, narrative analysis, or discourse analysis. It's imperative you pick the right tools for the job, as trying to hammer a screw into wood won't get you anywhere.

Familiarizing yourself with scales of measurement is another fundamental step—from nominal, ordinal, interval, to ratio scales, each comes with its unique flavours and seasoning for your analytical cookbook. Why does this matter? Because the type of scale you're dealing with directly influences the statistical tests you can legitimately use (Sullivan & Artino, 2013).

Descriptive statistics are your best friends in the data analysis playground. They're the helpful folks that summarize and describe the essence of your data points in a digestible form. Measures like mean, median, and mode for quantitative data or content analysis for qualitative data allow you to grasp the overall shape of your findings before diving deeper.

But it's not just about what the data shows—it's equally about what it doesn't. You'll want to consider variability, standard deviation, and the range for quantitative datasets. For qualitative data, consider the variability in contexts, perspectives, and depth of responses. Can't stress this enough, variations and outliers can sometimes tell you more than the trend itself.

Causality and correlation also play pivotal roles in data analysis. Just because two variables seem to dance together doesn't mean one leads the other—and you'll need to discern this carefully in your study (Sullivan & Artino, 2013). Statistical tests can help, but it's your critical thinking that truly untangles the web of causality.

Inferential statistics allow you to make predictions or inferences about a larger population based on a sample. It gives you the power to reach beyond your data without overextending—generalization, when done properly, can elevate your study from a local affair to one of broader relevance (Creswell & Creswell, 2017).

And then there's reliability and validity, the hallmark of quality data analysis. Reliability means consistency—can someone else whip up the same dish following your recipe? Validity is about accuracy—does your delicious-looking dish taste as good as it appears? Are you truly measuring what you aimed to measure?

Conceptualizing and operationalizing your variables is also a crucial step you can't overlook. It's like knowing the difference between table salt and kosher salt—a seemingly insignificant distinction that can significantly affect your results. Making sure you're measuring your concepts accurately is as vital as salt is to a dish—it brings out the flavor and can make or break your dish, I mean, dissertation (Creswell & Creswell, 2017).

With a grasp on these fundamentals, the path to more complex analyses, whether quantitative or qualitative, becomes less intimidating. Techniques like regression analysis, path analysis, or content analysis may seem daunting, but they are simply built on these basic principles.

As we move towards interpreting results in the next section, keep in mind that analysis isn't just a mechanical process—it requires intuition, creativity, and, yes, occasionally the bravery to say "the data just isn't giving us what we predicted." That, my friend, takes as much skill and scholarly rigor as crunching the numbers does.

To sum up, your toolkit for data analysis fundamentals should be equipped with a thorough understanding of your data types, measurement scales, descriptive and inferential statistics, concepts of reliability and validity, and the proper conceptualization of variables. Keep honing this toolkit as you analyze, interpret, and present your data—the feast of findings you serve up will be all the more satisfying for it.

Interpreting Results

The data's been crunched and the numbers have settled. You stare at your results, and a tinge of excitement—or perhaps it's dread—flutter in your belly. This is the moment of truth, where we dig beneath the surface. Interpreting your results isn't just a matter of 'what' the data shows, but the 'so what' and 'now what' of your findings. It's the bridge connecting your data to your research questions and the broader scope of your field. Let's demystify this beast, shall we?

First, let's get grounded. When you interpret results, you're not just summarizing the data; you are providing an explanation of what the data means in the context of your research (Bryman, 2016). This involves making inferences about the relationships among variables and fitting your findings into the existing framework that you've mapped out in your literature review.

Begin the interpretation by revisiting your research questions or hypotheses. Align each result with the respective question it addresses.

Ask yourself, do the findings answer the question? How do they answer it? This direct comparison ensures you keep the discussion relevant and avoid falling into the trap of tangential ramblings that lose sight of your research objectives.

Now, let's talk differences and significance. If your data shows varying results between groups or over time, you must articulate these differences meaningfully. Don't just state that 'Group A scored higher than Group B,' but dig into the 'why.' What do these differences suggest about the phenomenon you're studying? If using quantitative methods, consider the statistical significance of your results. Don't shy away from letting readers know whether a finding was unexpected and explore potential reasons for it.

The importance of context can't be overstressed. Layer your results with the context of the environment in which the data was gathered (Maxwell, 2013). Think about how external variables, not controlled for in your study, might've influenced outcomes. If studying human behavior, for instance, consider cultural, economic, or social factors that might play a role.

Let's not forget qualitative data. Interpretation here is less about numbers and more about patterns, themes, and narratives (Creswell & Creswell, 2017). Your job is to weave coherent stories from these narratives, always tying them back to your research questions. Look for overarching themes that emerged, discuss their significance, and don't just cherry-pick quotes that align with your expectations—address the contradictions as well.

Once you've dealt with the immediate findings, you should contemplate their implications. Simply put, what do these results mean for the field? How do they advance our understanding, and where do they slot into the existing body of knowledge? A single study is but a puzzle piece; your task is to show how it fits into the broader picture, perhaps challenging or expanding what's currently known.

Comparing and contrasting your findings with previous studies is invaluable. However, resist the urge to merely list comparisons. Go deeper by discussing why your results might align or differ from past research. Consider methodology, sample differences, and the time of study as potential factors.

What about anomalies? Don't sweep them under the rug. Anomalies, outliers, or unexpected patterns could be the most intriguing part of your analysis. Discuss these openly; they can reveal limitations of your study or point to areas for further research.

As you conclude the interpretation, reflect on the limitations of your study and how they could influence the findings. No study is perfect. Acknowledging limitations doesn't diminish your research but rather shows critical thinking and enhances credibility. Plus, it paves the way for future studies to build on your work.

Lastly, consider the practical implications of your findings. Are there actionable recommendations for practitioners, policymakers, or other stakeholders in your field? Don't leave your readers hanging with a 'so what'—give them a 'thus, you might consider this' instead.

When you wrap up this epic analysis saga, you need to craft the narrative in such a manner that leads readers through a journey of discovery, clearly articulating the significance of your results at every turn. Your interpretation should be the final love letter to your data—respectful of its nuances and mindful of its place in the grand scheme of things.

So, take a deep breath, put on your analytical cap, and approach your results with a healthy mix of skepticism, curiosity, and excitement. Your interpretation is the soul of your dissertation, infusing life into numbers and trends, transforming data into wisdom, and ultimately, contributing a speck of knowledge to the ocean of our collective understanding.

Software Tools for Analysis

As we delve into the realm of data analysis, you'll quickly notice that while your brain is the command center, your computer can be just as mighty with the right software. Now, you don't have to be a tech wizard to use these tools, but having a few solid ones under your belt can make a world of difference. They can help you crunch numbers, understand patterns and make sense of your research findings.

First off, let's talk about Quantitative data analysis. If numbers make you feel like you're reading ancient hieroglyphics, fear not! Statistic software like SPSS, SAS, or MATLAB can help translate. These powerful tools offer a range of statistical tests, from simple t-tests to complex multivariate analysis (Field, 2013). With a bit of practice and guidance, interpreting your data becomes less of a headache and more of an 'aha!' moment. SPSS is what I used for my research and I found many YouTube videos that explained in great detail how to use the program.

For the qualitative researchers in the house, coding data can seem like herding cats, and almost as much fun. But with programs like NVivo or Atlas.ti, you have catnip! These tools let you organize, categorize, and find connections in your text, audio, and video data. It's like having a super-assistant who never gets tired and loves detail.

When it's time to visualize your findings, which can add that extra pizzazz to your dissertation, consider Tableau or Microsoft Excel. They turn rows of data into clear, convincing graphs and charts that tell your story at a glance. Excel is likely familiar territory, but don't hesitate to venture into Tableau, which can handle larger datasets and offers more sophisticated visualizations (Fry, 2014).

Let's not overlook reference management software. When you're knee-deep in literature, tools like Zotero, EndNote, or Mendeley can be lifesavers. They not only keep your sources organized but also make citation a breeze. Plus, they often integrate with word processors, which means less time formatting and more time analyzing (Henshall, 2019).

Now, some of you might be working with geospatial data or GIS. Here, software like ArcGIS or QGIS comes into play. These tools allow you to map and analyze spatial relationships, which can be a game changer for certain research topics. The best part? There's a community of fellow mappers out there, always ready to help a comrade in need.

If you're into the nitty-gritty of data mining or want to predict trends, software such as Python with its libraries (think pandas, NumPy, or SciPy) or R can be your oracle. Don't fret if you've never coded before; these communities are full of tutorials and forums to help you get on your feet (McKinney, 2017).

For the mixed-methods researchers juggling both qualitative and quantitative data, MAXQDA and Dedoose offer a very cool and useful solution. They support both data types, making it easier to triangulate your findings and paint a more comprehensive picture of your research landscape.

Now, collaboration is another aspect you can't ignore. Dropbox, Google Drive, and OneDrive can become your virtual research hubs, where you and your advisor or peers can exchange data, notes, and drafts effortlessly – well, as long as your Wi-Fi doesn't bail on you.

Lastly, let's chat about project management tools – because, let's face it, analysis is just one scene in the epic movie of your dissertation. Trello, Asana, or Microsoft Project can help you keep track of your progress, keeping you and your deadlines in sync. Google calendar is also very useful. Enter all of your important due dates in Google Calendar as it is available on most smart phones.

All these tools amount to an arsenal that can dramatically improve the quality and efficiency of your analysis. However, the key is choosing the right weapon for your particular research battle. Always assess your needs, the learning curve, and of course, your budget before making a decision.

Remember, using these tools will require a learning investment upfront, but that time can pay off in spades when it comes to interpreting your results and drawing insights. Moreover, they can contribute to the reproducibility of your research, an aspect increasingly valued in scientific inquiry (Peng, 2011).

But beware! These software tools are just instruments – they're not doing the research for you. Your critical thinking skills are irreplaceable when it comes to assessing the output they provide. Always scrutinize the data, question the results, and remember that software is an aide, not a substitute for your intellectual rigor.

In conclusion, while the thought of taming these software beasts may initially seem daunting, don't be intimidated. With a dash of courage and a spoonful of perseverance, these tools can transform you into an analysis ninja, slicing through your data with precision and clarity. And as you embark on this journey, remember that these tools are meant to be your allies, working alongside you to unravel the story that your data is waiting to tell.

Chapter 5:
Academic Writing Skills

Transitioning from the analytical rigor of data analysis, Chapter 5 dives into the heart of your dissertation journey—honing your academic writing skills. It's a craft, really, requiring a blend of clarity, precision, and a tinge of scholarly elegance. Imagine constructing a sturdy yet intricate bridge that spans the gap between your thoughts and the reader's understanding. That's what you're doing here. Writing at this level isn't just about slapping words on a page; it's about sculpting your findings and arguments into a coherent narrative that flows as smoothly as a conversation with an old friend. You'll need to grasp the nuances of structuring your dissertation to guide your reader effortlessly through your research journey. We're talking about building a framework that supports your insights while adhering to the rigors of academic excellence. Plus, you've got to master the scholarly tone and style that whispers credibility to your audience (and whispers sweet nothings to your review committee). And let's not pretend—writer's block can hit like a freight train at the worst possible times, but fear not; this chapter will equip you with strategies to break through that wall with the finesse of a seasoned writer. So grab your pen, or better yet, position your hands over that keyboard, and let's get those academic writing muscles in shape. With that, your ideas are about to come alive on the page, captivating the minds and sparking the curiosity of those who venture into your academic oeuvre.

Structuring Your Dissertation Finding a way to structure your dissertation might feel like trying to herd cats, but remember, there's a method even to the messiest parts of life. Your dissertation isn't just a heap of information; it's a finely-tuned argument, and structuring it correctly can make or break its success. Here, we're going to break down the essentials to give your dissertation the backbone it needs to stand tall in the academic community. The university I attended started students early in the process to create a basic structure for their dissertations. The structure was called 10 points. The ten points answered such questions as, what methodology will you use and what is your research question. The ten points would then be further developed and eventually became dissertation chapters and sections.

Let's start with the big picture. Your dissertation will typically be composed of several key sections: the introduction, literature review, methodology, results, discussion, conclusion, and references. Sometimes, you'll have appendices or other supplementary material, but that's the gist of it. Now, each section has its own special jazz, and getting the tune right is crucial.

The introduction is not just hello; it's the hook that grabs your reader's attention and lays out the What, Why, and How of your work. You'll introduce your research question here, explaining its significance and the gap in the research that your study is addressing (Booth, Colomb, & Williams, 2016). It's your opening act, so make it sparkle with clarity and purpose.

Next, you glide into the literature review, and it's more than a high-level summary. It's where you weave together previous research into a story that supports the necessity of your study. This requires critical thinking and the ability to synthesize information to show the trends and themes that emerge from the literature. It's all about setting the stage for your show-stopping work (Ridley, 2012).

Your methodology is your blueprint to replication. It outlines the design, participants, instruments, and procedure of your study.

Transparency is king here. Any other researcher should be able to read this and recreate your study exactly. Precision and attention to detail in this section save everyone a headache down the line (Creswell & Creswell, 2017).

Then comes the data analysis. Buckle up—just kidding, we don't buckle in this ride. But seriously, this section is about showcasing your findings in a logical and systematic manner. It's not just tables and figures; it's your interpretation of what those numbers mean in the context of your research question. It requires a balance of statistical expertise and narrative ability.

The discussion is where you let it all out. You'll interpret results, considering the implications of what you've found and comparing them to the theories and findings you discussed in your literature review. This is not just navel-gazing; it's a critical examination of your work in the broader field. Here, you also acknowledge your limitations without selling yourself short—a tricky dance.

The conclusion is your swan song. Tie it all together, reinforce the importance of your findings, and leave your audience with a sense of closure. Yet, it's also the place to suggest future research directions, keeping the conversation going even as you drop the mic.

References feel straightforward, but they're the bread crumbs leading back to your intellectual feast. Make sure they're formatted impeccably; this isn't the place for creative expression. Whether it's APA, MLA, or Chicago style, stick to one and be consistent.

Okay, so you've got your sections mapped out, but structuring isn't just about the order of things. It's also about the flow within each section. Transition sentences aren't just polite—they're essential. They guide your reader from one point to the next, making clear connections and maintaining the momentum of your argument (Silvia, 2014).

Each paragraph should be a self-contained unit of thought. Start with a topic sentence that states the main point, followed by supporting sentences with evidence, and finish with a concluding sentence that reflects on the significance of the paragraph in relation to your overall argument. Like a good playlist, each paragraph sets the tone for the next.

Visual aids are your friends. Tables, charts, and figures can illustrate your points more efficiently than words sometimes. But treat them like guests at a dinner party; they should contribute to the conversation, not dominate it. Furthermore, make sure each one is discussed in the text; they can't speak for themselves.

It's easy to play fast and loose with headings, but they're your framework. Headings and subheadings divide your work into digestible chunks. They're not just decorative; make them descriptive and uniform. Think of them as signposts that tell your readers what's coming up on the highway of your dissertation.

How do you manage consistency and ensure you're structuring effectively? Outlines are your lifeline. A good outline is like a storyboard for a film—it doesn't tell the whole story, but it does show you where you're going. Before you dive into the writing, plot out each section and subsection. What key points do you need to hit? How will you transition from one to the next? Outlining will save you from meandering down a path that doesn't lead to your final destination.

Finally, the appendices. If everything in the main body of your text is the meal, the appendices are the spice rack. Here you can stash detailed tables, questionnaires, consent forms, or anything else that's necessary but not central to the narrative of your dissertation. They're there if someone wants more detail, but they're not in the way of the main course.

In summary, structuring your dissertation requires a balance of creativity and strict adherence to academic conventions. It's about presenting your research in a clear, logical manner, while telling a compelling story. The goal is to make it as easy as possible for the reader to understand and be persuaded by your argument.

Scholarly Tone and Style is an aspect of academic writing that isn't just about dotting your i's and crossing your t's. It's an art form requiring a blend of precision, clarity, formality, and yes, a touch of accessibility. It's how you communicate your ideas to your academic peers while maintaining an air of professional credibility. Let's dive into the nuances of this essential writing style and how to wield it effectively in your dissertation.

In the realm of academia, the scholarly tone is your linguist's attire—always dressed to impress, yet appropriate for the occasion. It involves utilizing a formal vocabulary that's subject-specific. But it's not about throwing in complex words to sound smart; it's about accuracy (Hyland, 2005). Picture it like this: you wouldn't wear a ball gown to a coffee shop, similarly, don't use convoluted language when a simpler term would suffice and maintain meaning.

Style goes hand-in-hand with tone, like rhythm to a song. You want to ensure your writing flows logically with ideas that are clearly developed and connected. The trick here is structure. Like the backbone of any good argument, your dissertation needs a well-built skeleton – from your abstract down to your appendices. Stick to one idea per paragraph and make it dance smoothly to the next, transitioning with precision and purpose (Swales & Feak, 2012).

Clarity is king, or in less regal terms, make sure you can't be misunderstood. Active voice often cuts through confusion better than passive, but don't treat it like an absolute rule. Sometimes, especially when highlighting the action over the actor, passive voice fits just right (Gopen & Swan, 1990). You're painting a picture with words, and each sentence you lay down is a brushstroke in your scholarly masterpiece.

Objectivity is another pillar of your scholarly tone. It doesn't mean stripping your work of all personality—far from it. It means presenting arguments and evidence without letting personal bias turn your dissertation into a soapbox. You're more a reporter than a columnist in this draft; let your findings speak for themselves.

Citations are your academic trust signals; they show you've done your homework. They are also a minefield for errors. Stick to APA style, as that's the currency of academic exchange, and make sure every fact is accounted for with an academic source. It's meticulous, yes, but accuracy in attribution is non-negotiable for scholarly work.

Precision in language cannot be overstated. Words have power, particularly in academic writing, and every term you select carries weight. Nuance can alter meaning, and academic arguments hinge on these subtleties. Scope out your lexicon carefully, and choose words that carry the exact shade of meaning you intend (Orwell, 1946).

Complexity in sentence structure can enrich your writing, adding layers and texture to your scholarly narrative. Don't shy away from compound or complex sentences to frame sophisticated ideas. However, temper this with simplicity where it enhances understanding. A labyrinthine sentence that loses the reader serves no one.

Consistency in your writing guarantees a smooth read. If you choose a term for a concept, stick with it throughout your dissertation to avoid confusion. Also, maintain a consistent tense to provide temporal clarity. If your study is completed, past tense is your go-to. Present tense can suggest an ongoing dialogue or current relevance.

Humility in your writing recognizes the broader academic conversation. Acknowledge the giants on whose shoulders you stand, yet understand it's your turn to contribute. Be confident but not boastful, and acknowledge the limitation of research with grace and professionalism.

Engagement with the reader is a subtle balance in scholarly writing. You're not crafting a thriller, but you don't want a snooze fest either. Dedicate time to connecting the dots for your reader; use examples to illustrate concepts and questions to provoke thought, guiding them through your research like a seasoned storyteller.

The scholarly tone and style can't be an afterthought; it has to be baked into your writing process. Think of your first draft as a block of marble, and subsequent revisions are where you chisel away, refining your tone and style until you reveal the David within your dissertation.

Critiques and peer reviews are not just a hoop to jump through, but a crucible for your writing. Embrace them. Let the feedback temper your work, strengthening your tone and style. Your peers are invaluable in helping you hone a pitch-perfect scholarly voice.

Bias in language is a pitfall to avoid. Your choice of words can unintentionally convey bias. Be mindful of inclusive language and rid your dissertation of any phrasing that could be interpreted as discriminatory or prejudiced—a scholarly misstep you can't afford to make.

Finally, remember that scholarly tone and style are not static. They evolve with the conventions of your discipline and the development of your own academic voice. Stay abreast of current standards in academic writing, and let your style mature as you deepen your expertise and understanding within your field.

With a conscientious approach to scholarly tone and style, your dissertation will stand as a testament to your hard work, critical thinking, and academic integrity. It's your voice in the academic choir—make sure it resonates with clarity, precision, and authority.

Overcoming Writer's Block

As you dig deeper into crafting your dissertation, there's a familiar foe many graduate students confront: writer's block. It's that wall you hit, where words don't flow and ideas seem to halt. But let's not despair – there are strategies to bulldoze that wall and get the creative academic juices flowing again. I had writer's block several times, but was able to overcome it by reading other dissertations and studies in my field.

Firstly, understand that writer's block is perfectly normal. It's not a sign of failure or lack of skill. Often, it's your brain's way of telling you it needs a break or a change of pace (Boice, 1994). It's essential to listen to these signals and to respond with kindness to yourself. Take short, frequent breaks – stand up, stretch, or go for a stroll. Give your mind some space so new ideas can blossom.

Secondly, try the "free writing" technique. Set a timer for 10-15 minutes and write without stopping, without worrying about grammar, style, or even making sense. This exercise can unclog your thoughts, and in the jumble of words, you might discover a gem to kickstart your formal writing (Elbow, 1998). I did this exercise many times and it worked beautifully.

Allotted time for writing can also work wonders. Designate specific periods of your day solely to writing, even if it's in short increments like the Pomodoro Technique suggests – work for 25 minutes, then rest for 5. This can help you create a rhythm and maintain a structured approach to writing, so you're not facing an endless, daunting task (Cirillo, 2006).

An outline is a powerful tool too. Even if you feel stuck, outlining the structure of your chapter or section can keep you moving. It doesn't need to be exhaustive – just a skeleton that guides you through the main points you wish to address. This can reduce the overwhelming feeling of creating substantial content from nothing.

Another tactic is to switch projects. When one aspect of your dissertation is making you hit a wall, alternate to a different chapter or even a separate, non-academic activity. This shift can reset your cognitive pathways and help you engage with the material from a refreshed perspective (Phillips & Pugh, 2015).

Talking about your research with a peer or even explaining it to someone unfamiliar with the topic can also aid in overcoming writer's block. This vocal processing can help you organize your thoughts and clarify your focus, allowing you to approach your writing with renewed clarity.

Remember too that your first draft doesn't have to be perfect. It's called a 'draft' for a reason. Permit yourself to write poorly at first and refine later. The act of writing, even badly, can propel you forward and provide material to sculpt and improve (Elbow, 1998).

Also, don't underestimate the power of reading. Taking time to read relevant literature can re-engage your analytical brain and provide inspiration. When you read, you're actively participating in the scholarly conversation that your dissertation will contribute to.

Sometimes, writer's block signals the need for more research. If you find yourself unable to write about a particular aspect of your dissertation, it might be because you need a deeper understanding of the topic. Returning to the research phase can fill in the gaps and bolster your confidence in writing about the subject (Phillips & Pugh, 2015).

Lastly, mental and physical health are critical in combating writer's block. Ensure you're getting ample sleep, eating nutritious foods, and engaging in physical activity. A healthy body fosters a sound mind, which in turn supports the cognitive demands of writing a dissertation.

Managing writer's block demands a multifaceted approach that considers your well-being, the flexibility of your writing practices, and the way you structure your work. By applying these strategies, you'll be well on your way to a fluid writing process that advances your dissertation effectively.

Remember, every writer faces this block at some point. What distinguishes a successful dissertation writer is not the absence of obstacles, but the strategies to overcome them. So, apply these techniques, stay committed to your work, and watch as those walls crumble to pave the way for your academic contributions to shine.

Chapter 6:
The Peer Review Process

If you've ever felt like the peer review process is akin to sending your carefully crafted dissertation through a gauntlet of scholarly scrutiny, you're not far off. It's the academic world's equivalent of a trust fall—relying on your peers to catch the weaknesses you've overlooked and prop up your research's integrity. The peer review process is a vital checkpoint that can make or break your work's acceptance into the realm of credible academic discourse (Mullins & Kiley, 2002). It's where the rubber meets the road, as reviewers pore over your methodology, analysis, and arguments with a fine-toothed comb. Their critical eyes can't help but zero in on the nuances that need sharpening, the gaps begging for more evidence, and the arguments that aren't quite as airtight as you thought. The process, let me tell you, isn't for the faint-hearted. It requires a thick skin and an open mind, as you'll need to digest and incorporate feedback that may initially sting but is meant to strengthen your work in the long run (Tinkler & Jackson, 2004). With each iteration, your dissertation becomes more robust and refined, inching closer to the polished gem it's destined to be. So take a deep breath, and lean into the process; it's an academic rite of passage that inevitably leads to a better end product—the diploma-worthy dissertation you're aiming for (Lillis & Curry, 2010).

Preparing for Peer Review involves more than just crossing your fingers and hoping for the best. You've put your heart into this dissertation, and the thought of someone taking a red pen to it might feel like an imminent storm cloud over your sunny day. But let's be real—the process is all about making your work the polished gem it deserves to be. So let's dive in headfirst and figure out how to get you swimming through peer review like a pro.

First things first, before sending your dissertation to peers, give it a thorough self-review. Be your own critic. Hunt down any typos, discrepancies, or loose ends in arguments (Thompson, 2019). It's a bit like cleaning your house before the cleaning service comes over—you want them to focus on the deep clean, not the socks lying around. Read through your entire work with fresh eyes, maybe even pretend you're reading someone else's research; this can help you spot errors you were previously blind to.

After the self-assessment marathon, it's time to focus on your dissertation's structure. Remember, your peers are not mind-readers; they won't know where you intended to place that chart that somehow ended up three chapters away from its call-out. Scrutinize your document's organization. Are your chapters flowing as smoothly as a mountain stream? Do your sections build upon one another logically (Davis & Parker, 1997)? Good structure doesn't just happen; you need to mold it with intention.

Now, let's talk about consistency, because if your paper switches between different citation styles or flips from metric to imperial measurements like a tourist trying to figure out temperatures abroad, your reviewers are in for a bumpy ride. Stick to one style. The same goes for terminology and tone. You wouldn't wear a tuxedo to one chapter of your dissertation and board shorts to another, would you? The cohesion will save your reviewers from unnecessary confusion (Hawkins, 2021).

In the grand tradition of science, back up your claims with evidence. Your assertions should stand on a solid bedrock of data or scholarly discussion, not on shaky assumptions. Before you pass your paper off, double-check your references. Are they credible? Are they current? Scholars love to sink their teeth into outdated or obscure references, so make sure yours can withstand the scrutiny (Nguyen, 2020).

Remember, peer review is not a solo trip. Reach out to colleagues or mentors who are familiar with your field. Their insight can be invaluable, and they might catch blind spots you've glossed over (Hawkins, 2021). A dissertation is a communal effort in a way. It's your name on the cover, but a slice of wisdom from your community can be the secret sauce that takes it from great to outstanding.

That leads us to another cornerstone of preparation: alignment with your research objectives. Go through your dissertation with the primary question, "Does this section support my central research goal?" You've been living and breathing this research for so long that it's easy to go on tangents. Nip those in the bud. Your reviewers will thank you for a focused and directed read that doesn't wander off into the wilderness.

Then there's the matter of clarity. Clarity is kind. Your reviewers are busy folks with their hands full of their own research. Don't make them wade through a marsh of convoluted language and complex sentences. Write clearly, directly, and concisely. Where possible, simplify. This doesn't mean dumb it down—it means making your advanced concepts accessible and digestible (Davis & Parker, 1997).

The practical side of preparing for peer review includes formatting. Like an attentive butler, formatting silently works in the background to make sure everything is in its proper place. Follow your institution's template or the common standards in your field. Whichever you choose, apply it religiously throughout your manuscript—this is about creating a professional and polished appearance.

Anticipate criticism. It's going to happen. Part of revving up for review is bracing yourself for the feedback (good, bad, and ugly) and resolving to use it constructively. Remember, your reviewers are not your adversaries; they are your allies in pursuit of academic rigor. There's no room for defensiveness—only room for growth.

Protection against misinterpretation is also critical. Your reviewers can't read your mind, so make sure your writing doesn't require psychic abilities to understand. Explicitly state the significance of your research, your methodology, and your findings. Ensure that each of your points is supported so that it doesn't fall through gaping holes of ambiguity (Nguyen, 2020).

Now, let's think about the bigger picture for a moment. Reviewers also want to see the impact of your work—how it stands shoulder to shoulder with existing research and carves a path forward. Convey why your dissertation matters, both in the academic community and to the wider world, if applicable. Frame your work within the larger tapestry of human knowledge.

Your toolkit for preparing for peer review should also include a healthy dose of ethics. That's right—you need to ensure that your study and its reporting are ethically sound, from participant consent to data handling practices. Any unethical oversight could prove catastrophic, not only for the review process but for your reputation (Thompson, 2019).

Finally, respect the clock. Don't rush your review preparation. An undercooked meal doesn't do well at a potluck, and an underprepared dissertation won't do well in peer review. Give yourself plenty of time to prepare, revise, and polish. The more thorough you are now, the smoother the review process will be.

And there you have it—a practical guide to navigating the peer review waters. Remember, peer review is a rite of passage in the world of academic research, a baptism by fire that can fortify your work and sharpen your scholarly abilities.

Responding to Feedback is a crucial phase in the dissertation process that can either polish your gem of a study or scuff it up, depending on how you approach it. After pouring your heart, soul, and possibly countless cups of coffee into your research, it can feel like a personal attack when a reviewer lays out a buffet of critiques. But let's get one thing crystal clear: feedback is not about you, it's about the work. And the mission, if you dare to accept it, is to transform that critique into a stronger, more robust dissertation.

In this crucible of academic development, the first course of action is to detach your ego and emotions from the document. Picture your dissertation as a living thing; it's evolving. It's not personal when a reviewer dissects your methodology or questions your analysis—it's an opportunity for growth. Embrace feedback as a gift, albeit sometimes a sharply wrapped one that's poking you in the ribs, nudging your scholarly project towards excellence (Hattie & Timperley, 2007).

Parsing through comments, it's helpful to prioritize. Some feedback will be low-hanging fruit—typographical errors, formatting issues, maybe the odd citation gone astray. Make these corrections first to build momentum. Nothing feels quite as satisfying as seeing a slew of tracked changes turn from blood red to clean white on your manuscript. But don't get too carried away marking 'Resolved' on your document like a gunslinger at a Wild West showdown; some changes need a more considerate approach.

Now comes the heavy lifting. Let's talk content. You'll encounter feedback that feels like a Gordian knot, complex and intimidating. Break these down. Do you need to clarify your research question? Is there a flaw in your methodology? Are your conclusions overstated? These are not quick fixes—they're puzzles that require a cup of tea, a deep breath, and a thorough reassessment of your work. Approach these larger issues with a problem-solving mindset, and remember, sometimes your advisors or reviewers see things from an angle you haven't considered.

That being said, just because feedback is given, does not mean it must be taken. You are, after all, the expert in your tiny corner of the universe that is your dissertation topic. If a piece of feedback doesn't resonate, prepare to justify why your approach is valid. Articulate your rationale, back it up with literature, and if needed, gather more data to solidify your position. However, tread carefully; this isn't a hill to die on—you're crafting a scholarly argument, not mounting a defense at the Alamo.

Collaboration is key. A meeting with your advisor or even a fellow grad student for a fresh perspective can shine a light on what feels like an insurmountable issue. These conversations can produce the 'aha' moments that propel you beyond the sticking points (Mullins & Kiley, 2002). Just remember, you're the conductor of this symphony—others may guide you with their instruments, but in the end, the music is yours to direct.

Speaking of direction, there will be times when you're clueless about how to address a particular piece of feedback. That's normal. Take your time with it. It's like untangling a pair of earbuds; it seems impossible at first, but with patience and persistence, the knots loosen. Review literature, consider alternate viewpoints, and sometimes, put it away and sleep on it. Fresh eyes in the morning can bring new solutions.

Documentation is also crucial when responding to feedback. Keep track of the changes you make and the rationale behind them. Whether you're using a simple spreadsheet or a more sophisticated project management tool, having a record to refer back to can be invaluable, particularly when multiple rounds of revision start to blur together (Aitchison et al., 2010).

As you sift through the feedback, you'll start to feel the edges of your dissertation sharpening, the arguments tightening, the content solidifying. This is good; it means the process is working. It also means that you're nearing the crest of the hill where the protective umbrella of your committee begins to recede, and the broader academic community awaits. They'll have their own thoughts and critiques, a sign that your work is engaging others in scholarly dialogue.

Remember, perfect is not the goal—there's no such thing in research. The aim is to make your dissertation defensible, coherent, and reflective of a scholarly piece of work that adds value to the field. Feedback isn't a barricade; it's a series of checkpoints, ensuring your research journey doesn't veer off course. So instead of dreading those comments, welcome them as mile markers on your road to a successful defense.

In the end, how you respond to feedback may very well define your growth as a scholar. Like a good wine, your dissertation will improve with each revision. It's a grind, but it's also the craft of academia—polishing and refining ideas until they shine. Your dissertation is your magnum opus at this stage of your academic career, but it's just the beginning of a lifelong endeavor of inquiry, learning, and contributing to the ever-expanding universe of knowledge.

As the saying goes, Rome wasn't built in a day, and neither is a standout dissertation. Take the feedback, piece it together brick by brick, and watch as your research fortress stands tall, ready for the final defense and beyond. The reviewers aren't your enemies; they're your unwitting allies, challenging you to raise the bar and leap over it.

So, to recap: take a step back, prioritize, engage with the feedback critically but also with an open mind, collaborate, document, reflect, and refine. It's a process that, when followed diligently, can elevate your work from a mere requirement for a degree to a piece of scholarship that can truly make an impact (Smith & McGannon, 2018).

Now that you've got the tools to deal with feedback head-on, it's time to revisit your manuscript. The next section will guide you through the art of revisions. Each suggestion, each comment, and each change are threads in the tapestry of your research— weave them carefully.

Revising Your Dissertation

So, you've weathered the storm of writing your first draft, confronted the swell of data, and emerged with a dissertation that's just about ready to see the light of day—or so you might think. Hold onto your hats, because now comes the critical process of revising your dissertation (Boote & Beile, 2005). Like a sculptor refining a piece of marble, your academic masterpiece will require patience, precision, and a keen eye for detail to reach its full potential.

First and foremost, if you haven't already, take a bit of a breather. Distance from your work can provide a fresh perspective that is essential for effective revision. Once you've had some time to recharge those brain cells, approach your draft with a critical, discerning eye. You're not just correcting grammar here; you're overhauling arguments, tightening up your structure, and elevating your scholarly voice.

Take it one chapter at a time, and as you do, ask the big-picture questions: Does the chapter contribute to the overall argument? Is there a clear thread that connects all your chapters? These questions will guide you in ensuring that your dissertation is coherent and logically structured (Locke, Spirduso, & Silverman, 2020).

Transitioning from big-picture to the specifics, consider the clarity and flow of your prose. Fine-tune your sentences to ensure they are concise and direct. Examine each paragraph for a clear topic sentence and ensure that every subsequent sentence supports that main idea. If it doesn't, it's time to trim the fat.

Furthermore, scrutinize your citations and references. Every statement that is not your original thought needs a citation, and this isn't just busywork—it's a vital component of academic integrity (APA, 2020). Ensuring your references are correctly formatted not only respects the work of others but also bolsters your credibility as a researcher.

Another major aspect of revision is responding to feedback. If you've already gone through a peer review, lay out the feedback you've received. Approach criticism with an open mind—it's not personal, it's a path to improvement. Prioritize the suggestions, tackling the most substantial issues first (those related to your arguments, framework, or methodology) before moving on to the smaller, more manageable comments.

Don't work in a vacuum. Engage with your advisor or committee members during this process. Their seasoned eyes will catch issues you might not see and provide guidance grounded in experience. This collaborative process can help refine your thinking and clarify your dissertation's direction (Boote & Beile, 2005).

Bear in mind the importance of consistency. This includes maintaining a consistent tone and style throughout your dissertation. If your writing in earlier chapters is formal and academic, the latter chapters should follow suit. Review each section for uniformity in voice and tense, ensuring that your arguments maintain a steady tempo and tone from start to finish.

Don't overlook the seemingly trivial aspects such as formatting; adherence to your institution's guidelines is compulsory. Scrutinize your document's pagination, headings, tables, and figures for compliance. These elements may seem minor, but they contribute to the professional appearance and readability of your dissertation.

While revision is undoubtedly detailed work, it's also an iterative process. Don't expect to catch everything on the first go. Plan for multiple rounds of revisions to incrementally refine your dissertation (Locke et al., 2020). Each pass through the document is an opportunity to spot new details and improve sections you might have thought were already polished.

Keep track of the changes you make. Some researchers find it useful to maintain a revision log or a detailed list with notes explaining each significant change. This documentation can be invaluable, not just for your own record-keeping but also when you need to explain your revisions to your committee or in future peer-review processes.

As you revise, also remember to maintain your objectivity. It's easy to become attached to certain sentences or paragraphs that you've crafted with care. However, if they do not serve the overall argument or are redundant, they need to go. Revising is as much about cutting and condensing as it is about expanding and elucidating.

Don't hesitate to seek the support of other resources as well. Writing centers, workshops, or editors specializing in academic work can provide outside perspective and expertise that catalyze the revision process. Sometimes a new set of eyes can catch the errors that have become invisible to you.

In the end, remember that revising is an essential part of academic writing. It's the stage where your dissertation morphs from a draft full of potential to a polished piece of scholarship that's ready to contribute to the greater academic conversation. Embrace the revision process as an opportunity to learn, grow, and refine not just your dissertation but your own identity as a scholar.

Finally, when you think you have finished revising, give it another thorough read. Often, it is in this final pass where you'll find the small inconsistencies or lingering errors that escaped earlier detection. Patience is your ally; a meticulously revised dissertation is not only a requirement for your graduation but also a testament to your dedication and scholarly excellence (APA, 2020).

Chapter 7:
Crafting a Compelling Discussion

In the grand adventure that is your dissertation, landing at Chapter 7 means it's time to weave together the threads of your arguments, your data, and your jaw-dropping insights into a rich tapestry. That's right, we're diving into the heart of your research—crafting a discussion that not only resonates with your audience but also underlines your scholarly prowess. You've collected your data, you've analyzed it, and now you're staring at the beast that is the discussion section, wondering how to tame it. Fear not! This chapter is your trusty guide to making sure that your discussion isn't just a rehash of your results, but a dynamic conversation that connects the dots between your findings and the big picture questions you posed at the outset. You'll learn how to artfully link your results back to your hypothesis, turning what could be dry recitations of fact into a convincing narrative that even skeptics can't ignore. Sure, addressing limitations might feel like airing your dirty laundry, but it's actually your secret weapon for showcasing your critical thinking skills and understanding of the research process. Plus, by pinpointing exactly where future research could go based on your work, you're essentially passing the baton to the next generation of eager minds, and what's more fulfilling than that? This chapter is where your study comes full circle, and we'll make sure you cross that finish line with a discussion that packs a punch. So let's get down to the nitty-gritty and craft a discussion that'll have your committee nodding in agreement and your peers raising their glasses to your academic verve.

Linking Results to Your Hypothesis is a groove you've got to fit into just right; it's a dance where every step is a word, every spin is a sentence, with the music being your data hum. Here, it's not just about showing what you found; it's about tying those findings back to the big "Why" you started with, making a seamless tapestry from question to conclusion.

So, you've run the gauntlet of data collection and analysis (those chapters should be dog-eared by now), and you're staring down a sea of results. Before getting carried away, anchor yourself back to that critical hypothesis, or set of hypotheses, you formulated at the beginning of your journey. Think of your hypothesis as the North Star guiding your analytical ship; it's the reference point you consistently navigate back to when you're lost at sea in your data.

Remember, a hypothesis is essentially a prediction you've made based on your understanding of the subject (Kumar, 2019). Your results are now the moment of truth, the time to test whether your prediction holds water or not. And trust me, there's an art to this. You've got to approach it with the precision of a scientist, the simplicity of a storyteller, and the perspective of a critic all rolled into one.

Begin the link by explicitly reiterating the original hypothesis in the context of the results. Paint a clear before-and-after picture: "Before testing, I hypothesized that X would lead to Y. After a grueling battle with the numbers, here's what the data's telling us..." It's an origin story of your findings, curating a sense of journey for the reader, showing them where you've started and where you've landed. And if the data aligns with your hypothesis, fantastic—you're threading a needle with ease. But even if it doesn't, that's not the end. Science thrives on the unexpected, and so should you.

Let's say your hypothesis was proven wrong. Take a deep breath. This doesn't mean you've failed; it means you've learned something new, which is just as valuable. Dive into the discrepancies without defensiveness, probing into why your results might have sidelined your predictions. What were the assumptions that led you astray? How does the new info fit into the existing framework of understanding in your field (Maxwell, 2013)? Remember, every result is a stepping stone in the grand scheme of knowledge.

Then, turn on your storyteller's charm. Narrate the significance of these findings. Why should anyone care that Y didn't result from X, when everyone was so darn sure it would? Place your audience in the heart of the discovery, letting them feel the ripple of the implications. What does this mean for the field, for future research, for the real world? Even if your hypothesis was off, your findings might open doors you didn't even know existed.

It's also vital to link results not just to the hypothesis but to the literature you've so painstakingly reviewed. How does what you've unearthed align with or challenge the established research? Are there gaps in the literature that your study fills or deepens? Engaging in this discourse anchors your work within the scholarly community and gives it weight (Covey, 2004).

And as you're doing all this, keep it simple. Academic jargon might be tempting to slip into, as if complex words lend extra credibility to your work. They don't. Clarity and comprehension are your allies, and they will make your work accessible, which is ultimately what you want. So, while you weave this complex net of hypothesis and results, make sure it's not woven so tight that the sense can't shine through.

If you've used multiple hypotheses, tackle each one independently in this part of the dance. Give each their due spotlight, illustrating how each result relates back to the individual predictions. This helps maintain structure in your dissertation and makes it easier for your readers to follow the logical progression of your research findings.

Don't forget to pepper your exposition with the critical insight that Dr. Someone-or-other noted in their groundbreaking 2022 study. For instance: "Similar to the findings of Johnson et al. (2022), this research reveals a notable deviation from the conventional understanding of..." By referencing such studies, you reinforce the relationships between your work and existing research, supporting or refuting findings within the context of an academic dialogue.

Equally important is balancing humility and confidence. You've done the work, you know your stuff, but there's always room for growth and learning. Stating categorically that your results have proved your hypothesis might be overstepping; after all, in research, few things are ever proven with absolute certainty. It's more about supporting, suggesting, and associating your hypothesis with your findings. Use language that's confident yet tentative, presenting a sound case without overreaching.

How do you handle the complex statistical analyses or qualitative insights that informed your conclusions? One effective approach is to boil down the complexity into potent summaries. Transform stats and jargon into nuggets of wisdom that any determined reader, even one outside your field, can grasp. "What these numbers are really whispering is..." Think of it as translating data-dialect into common tongue.

Sometimes, you may find that your results spark new questions, creating a cascade effect of inquiry. Lean into this. It's the true spirit of research: a never-ending conversation where each answer spurs further questioning. Discuss these emerging inquiries within the context of your linked results and hypothesis, pitching your tent in the fertile ground of curiosity.

Now, as you polish this chapter, circling back to ensure your hypothesis and results are as snug as a bug in a rug, remember to keep your reader in mind. You're taking them by the hand, leading them through the logical labyrinth you've navigated, making sure each turn, each corner, is illuminated by explanation and evidence.

In the end, the exercise of linking your results to your hypothesis is more than a mere academic requirement; it's a narrative of your intellectual expedition, a testimony of your growth as a scholar, and a contribution to the continuum of knowledge. It's about stitching the fabric of your findings into the broader quilt of scientific inquiry, making sure your piece fits, stands out, and adds warmth to the collective understanding.

Addressing Limitations

So you've designed your study, gathered your data, and crunched the numbers. That's when the real fun begins, the part where humility meets science head-on: addressing the limitations of your research. Every dissertation, no matter how meticulously planned and executed, has its imperfections. There's a reason for that. Research is a human endeavor, and humans, by default, are not without flaw. The genius lies not in achieving perfection but in recognizing and accounting for these 'speed bumps' on the road to knowledge acquisition.

First, it's essential to understand that a limitation isn't a deadly flaw that blows your dissertation out of the water. Far from it. A well-handled limitation is a window into your intellectual honesty and rigor. Let's delve into identifying those limitations. They come in different flavors: methodological constraints, sample size restrictions, or limitations in the scope of your study, to name a few (Maxwell, 2020).

Methodological limitations can be tricky. Maybe you're doing qualitative work and your interpretive framework isn't a one-size-fits-all. Perhaps in a quantitative study, your sample size wasn't the army of participants you dreamt of but rather a platoon. That's not to say your findings aren't meaningful—they are—but they may not generalize to the whole population you're interested in. Recognizing this is key. It's like admitting your GPS occasionally loses the satellite signal. It doesn't mean you're lost; it just means you're admitting there are patches on your map that are a bit fuzzy (Silverman, 2017).

Then there's the scope of your research. You've focused on a specific angle, as you should have, but this means you can't claim to cover all bases. Your study might look at one aspect of a phenomenon, but not all the associated factors. It's like shining a spotlight on the stage; you illuminate one part while leaving others in shadow. Recognizing what's outside that beam of light is critical to understanding the reach and relevance of your study (Smith & Davis, 2019).

Now, how do you go about documenting these limitations? It's not about burying them in a footnote where no one will see. Incorporate limitations into the discussion section of your dissertation, addressing them head-on. Acknowledge the elephant in the room. It shows you understand your research, the broader context, and where your work fits into the grand tapestry of academic inquiry.

The best way to address limitations is by contextualizing them. Explain why they occurred and how they impact your findings. This transparency isn't weakness; it's a strength. It underscores the reliability and credibility of your work. And remember, every limitation is a signpost for future research. It's not a dead end; it's an invitation for you, or someone else, to pick up the baton and carry on the research journey (Thomas, 2022).

Consider triangulation to bolster the validity of your findings. Maybe your methodology has some weak spots, but by using different data sources, methods, or theories to cross-check information, you cover more bases. It's like checking the accuracy of your watch against others; if they all show the same time, you're probably on the mark (Maxwell, 2020).

When writing about limitations, balance is critical. Don't overemphasize them to the point of undercutting your work, but don't underplay them either. It's a tightrope walk between caution and confidence. You're not discrediting your study but rather giving it its due respect as a piece of a puzzle that's still being pieced together by the scholarly community.

That said, don't think of limitations as the ugly sidekick to your research questions. In fact, some could argue that articulating the limitations of your study is just as insightful as discussing your findings. It encourages critical thinking and ongoing dialogue, which, let's be honest, is the lifeblood of academic progress (Smith & Davis, 2019).

Lastly, address limitations in your defense with the composure of a seasoned captain steering through choppy waters. The examination committee will test your mettle, and they'll respect you more for navigating these challenges with poise and understanding. It's not about defending yourself against criticism; it's about demonstrating your capacity for reflective, critical research practice.

In sum, to address limitations seamlessly, identify them early, discuss them candidly, contextualize their implications, suggest how future research may overcome them, and keep a balanced perspective throughout. Doing so will not only enhance the solidity of your dissertation but will also earn you the respect of your peers and superiors in the academic arena.

And there you have it—a guide to embracing and addressing the limitations of your research with the skill of an academic ninja. Remember, it's these nuances that separate the novice researchers from the knowledgeable ones. Your dissertation is your launchpad, and acknowledging its limitations only adds fuel to your trajectory, shooting you into the realm of respected scholars.

Implications for Future Research

Skimming through the preceding chapters, you've armed yourself with the nuts and bolts of dissertation work, from ethical considerations to the thrill of the defense. But as you edged closer to the climax of this intellectual adventure, there's a lingering sensation that your work is far from done. It's not just about sealing a study with a satisfying conclusion; it's about setting the stage for the next act—the promising land of future research.

In the world of academia, every question answered often unravels several more, each itching for inquiry. When wrapping up your dissertation, ponder the untapped avenues that sprang from your study's findings. These unanswered questions and unresolved issues are your legacy, the breadcrumbs for the next generation of discovery seekers to follow.

Some may ask, "Why bother with future research implications?" Well, championing future research directions is an intellectual nudge to your peers. It says, "Here's a path less trodden," tempting the curious minds who dare to venture further. It's a critical component of scholarly contribution, ensuring that knowledge doesn't stagnate but flows like a relentless river.

Now, let's navigate the waters of suggesting future research. First thing, zero in on the gaps. No matter the thoroughness of your study, there's always a crevice that couldn't be filled—perhaps due to time constraints, resources, or the scope of your research. Identify these gaps and suggest how they can be explored further (Smith et al., 2021). For instance, if your study was confined to a particular geographic area or demographic, propose how future scholars can expand the research to new populations or settings.

Next, consider the methodological tweaks that could reveal new dimensions. Maybe you chose a qualitative approach, but quantitative methods could yield a different perspective—or vice versa. By recommending alternate methodologies or combinations thereof, you encourage a richer, more comprehensive understanding of the topic (Dawson, 2019).

In the same vein, ponder the theoretical frameworks that underpinned your study. Did your research challenge or support existing theories? Perhaps it unearthed new theoretical implications that deserve further scrutiny. Proposing theoretical explorations for future research can pave the way for profound shifts in your discipline (Adams & Lawrence, 2019).

While pondering over future research, don't skip over the tech tools that emerged during your study. Maybe during your data analysis, you dreamt of a software tool that would have simplified the process or offered more robust insights. Lay down the seeds for tech-savvy future researchers to develop or leverage upcoming technologies to tackle similar questions.

Reflect, too, on the broader societal and practical applications of your findings. If your research has implications for policy-making, healthcare, education, or any sector beyond academia, highlight how future research could hone these implications into actionable strategies that benefit society.

Now, let's not sugarcoat it—limiting factors will have had their say during your research. Maybe the budget was tighter than skinny jeans or the timeline as compressed as a college student's during finals week. Use your limitations section as a springboard to suggest deeper or broader exploration in a less constrained environment.

And hey, technology is advancing at a breakneck speed. By the time you've dotted the last i in your dissertation, some newfangled tech might just be emerging. Highlight how future research could capitalize on these emerging technologies to leapfrog over the hurdles you encountered.

Also, consider longevity. Research isn't a one-hit-wonder but a lifelong jam session. If your study has the potential for longitudinal research—a chance to track changes over time—cue the next batch of researchers to pick up where you left off and keep the records spinning.

Let's not forget the partnerships that could spring from your study. Maybe your research uncorked opportunities for cross-disciplinary work, where science meets humanities, or economics shakes hands with environmental studies. Underline these potential collaborations, and point to how different academic territories can come together for a mash-up that might just rock the scholarly world.

Facilitating replication studies is also key. Encourage others to test your findings under new conditions or with different variables. This not only fortifies the robustness of your results but also sparks off a wealth of data that can be mined by future scholars (Dawson, 2019).

Lest we forget the policy implications; if your study has the muscle to influence law, education policies, or any other set of rules governing human beans out there, spell out how further research could sculpt these areas. The bridge between ivory tower findings and the pavement pounded by policy can only be built with the blueprints you provide.

Lastly, wield reflection as a tool. Look back at your research journey with a scrutinizing lens, and consider how you could have approached it differently. Share these introspections as opportunities for future research, so the next wave of doctoral students can start their journey with a full quiver of strategies and a sharpened focus.

Through all this, keep a humble tone. Your dissertation won't be the Rosetta Stone of your field, and that's fine. The point is to contribute a piece to the ever-expanding puzzle of knowledge and invite others to keep building upon it.

In conclusion, paving the way for future research is as crucial as the study itself. It's about passing the baton gracefully, igniting the spark of curiosity in others, and keeping the bonfire of inquiry burning bright. Your dissertation is not just a culmination; it's a foundation for the endless constructions of knowledge yet to come.

Chapter 8:
Perfecting Your Presentation

As we pivot from structuring a bulletproof discussion in your dissertation to ensuring your verbal explanation packs just as much of a punch, Chapter 8 swings into the critical art of perfecting your presentation. Conveying your months or even years of hard work in a comprehensive and engaging way to a panel of academics isn't just about getting all your ducks in a row; it's about making them dance. You'll need to move beyond the familiarity of your written words to a presentation that resonates with clarity, confidence, and authority. Here, you'll learn to distill complex ideas into accessible and memorable bites that won't just meet the requirements of your dissertation committee but will captivate them. Crafting a narrative arc that threads through your slides will transform your presentation into an enlightening journey for your audience. No detail is too minute when rehearsing your defense, where tone, timing, and the ability to read the room can mean the difference between hurrahs and harrowing silences. And when those inevitable questions come flying, you'll be armed with strategies to tackle critiques with poise and thoughtful consideration. Remember, the strength of your research is as much in its scholarly rigor as it is in your ability to communicate it effectively (Rowley & Slack, 2004; Zerubavel, 1999). Stay tuned as we delve into the nuances of creating and delivering a presentation that will be remembered for all the right reasons.

Creating Impactful Slides As you transition from the craftsmanship of writing to the finesse of presenting, remember that your slides are the bridge between your scholarly work and your audience. In crafting slides for your dissertation defense, think of them as your visual soundtrack—each one should complement and enhance the narrative of your research journey without overshadowing it. This isn't just about showing off data; it's about story-telling in a way that clicks with your listeners.

Start by considering the overarching narrative of your dissertation. Your slides should follow the arc of this story, with each slide acting as a chapter marker guiding the audience through your research. It's like laying down a trail; you want to guide your audience along, providing signposts and clear directions so they don't get lost in the woods of data and methodology.

But let's not forget design, which is as critical as substance. Slides cluttered with text are the academic equivalent of a snooze button. Keep text to a minimum, bullet points crisp, and information digestible. Remember, your slides are there to support your oral narrative, not replace it. Think of them as billboards along a highway—your audience should be able to 'drive by' and catch the key message at speed (Mayer & Moreno, 2003).

Now, let's address the visual components. Graphics, charts, and images should be more than just pretty pictures; they have to pack a punch. This means selecting images that resonate with your content and using charts that clearly present your data without requiring a magnifying glass to decipher (Tufte, 2001). It's a delicate balance—enough detail to back your claims, but not so much that your slide becomes a data cemetery.

Color can be your ally or your foe. Use it wisely to draw attention or to categorize, but resist the carnival approach. You're not throwing a fiesta; you're aiming for a scholarly conversation. Opt for a cohesive and professional color scheme that won't distract or disorient your viewers.

Let's not forget about the textual content. Fonts may seem trivial, but they're the clothes your words wear. Choose fonts that are easy on the eyes and big enough to be seen from the back of the room. Your choice of font and size can affect readability and the perceived professionalism of your presentation (Tufte, 2001).

Now, consider the structure of your content on each slide. Just throwing bullet points onto a slide will not cut it. Instead, aim to tell a story with the flow of information. Structure your slides in a way that leads the viewer through your findings step by step, building a case that's irrefutable by the time you reach the climax—your research conclusions.

Transitions and animations can be the spice of a presentation, but they can just as easily be its downfall. Use them sparingly and with purpose. Every zoom, fade, or swipe should have a clear rationale behind it. Done right, transitions can guide attention and emphasize points. Done wrong, they become the visual version of stuttering (Mayer & Moreno, 2003).

When it comes to sharing complex data or models, simplicity becomes your superpower. Break down complicated concepts into easier-to-digest segments. If you're discussing a multifaceted diagram, consider introducing it in stages rather than revealing the full labyrinth in one go.

Consistency should be the heartbeat of your slides. This means sticking to a limited set of fonts, colors, and slide layouts. Jumping from one design to another can disorient your audience more than a sudden plot twist in a complex novel. You want your presentation to feel like a well-curated gallery, not a random assortment at a yard sale.

But here's the rub: A phenomenal slide deck doesn't guarantee an equally phenomenal presentation. It's not just about what's on your slides; it's even more about how you use them. Practice pacing your narrative with your slides. The slides are your sidekick, not the superhero of the show. You should be stealing the spotlight, not the other way around.

Accessibility should also be on your mind. Not everyone experiences the world in the same way, so account for this in your slide design. Ensure your presentations can be followed by individuals with color blindness or other visual impairments (Alley & Neeley, 2005).

Lastly, be ready to jump ship if needed. Technology has a notorious reputation for failing when it's most crucial. Have a backup plan in case of technical difficulties. Know your material well enough to present without your visual aids, or have printed copies on hand as a failsafe. This preparation shows professionalism and composure under pressure.

In putting together impactful slides, encapsulate the essence of your research without overcomplicating. It's an exercise in precision and restraint. With every slide, ask yourself, 'Does this add to my story? Is it clear, concise, and compelling?' If the answer is no, it's time to go back to the drawing board. Your slides are your silent partners in the quest to convince, and when wielded well, they can make the difference between a good defense and a great one.

Remember, creating impactful slides is a craft that requires as much thought and planning as any other part of your dissertation journey. They should be tailored to your research, your style, and your message—all while being digestible, accessible, and technically fail-safe. With this in mind, you can create a set of slides that not only enhance your presentation but elevate it, leaving a lasting impression on your committee and your audience.

Rehearsing Your Defense Transitioning from the absorbing process of writing to the performance art of defending, we're at the juncture where all those long nights and endless edits finally pay off. Think of your defense rehearsal as a dress rehearsal in theater—it's where you work out the kinks, pace your narrative, and get comfortable with the spotlight. Securing a convincing defense isn't just about knowing your research inside and out; it's about conveying your knowledge in a way that's coherent, confident, and compelling.

First things first, you need to understand the format. What's the protocol for your institution? How long is your presentation supposed to be? Who will be in attendance? Get the logistics down pat, as these will shape your rehearsal process. You want to tailor your defense to the expectations of your committee and the rules of your academic institution (University of North Carolina at Chapel Hill, 2022).

After you've got the structural details sorted, build your narrative. How does your research flow? Can you tell a clear story from hypothesis to conclusion? Establish your opening statement as a hook that reels your committee in and gives a roadmap of your journey. Then move to elucidate each chapter of your dissertation, ensuring a smooth transition between each segment.

Visual aids are your allies, but they can also be your downfall if misused. Ensure your slides complement and highlight your talk, instead of overshadowing or duplicating it. Every visual should have a purpose (Clark, 2017). If a slide doesn't add clarity or impact to your narrative, it may be best to leave it out. This minimalist approach will keep your audience's attention focused on your storytelling.

Now, with the script in hand, it's time to practice, practice, and practice some more. Start by presenting to an empty room, then gradually up the stakes by inviting colleagues or your advisor to watch. Record yourself if possible—video doesn't lie, and it will be eye-opening to watch your own performance. Pay attention not just to what you say, but how you say it. Are you mumbling? Rushing? Using too many filler words? Iterative practice will iron these issues out.

Remember to practice your pacing. The best defenses are those that fit comfortably within the allotted time. It's about respect for your committee's schedule, and it demonstrates your ability to convey critical information efficiently. Run through your talk with a stopwatch, and if you're consistently running long, trim the fat off your presentation (University of Leicester, 2021).

During your rehearsal, simulate the defense's Q&A session. This is where many candidates stumble, not because they don't know their research, but because they're unprepared for the curveballs. Anticipate the tough questions, the weaknesses in your study, and practice clear, concise responses. Knowing the potential criticisms of your work can often transform them into discussions about the scope and implications for future research.

Dress rehearsal isn't the time to improvise your wardrobe choice either. Decide on your defense outfit in advance—something that strikes the balance between professional and comfortable. Feeling good in what you're wearing plays a part in your overall confidence. Plus, it removes one more variable from the big day that could distract you. I wore a suit during my defense.

Handling nerves is a non-negotiable skill here. Practicing relaxation techniques such as deep breathing, visualization, or mindfulness can play a major part in keeping jitters at bay (Association for Psychological Science, 2019). The more you rehearse, the more second nature your defense becomes - reducing anxiety and allowing you to think on your feet.

Don't underestimate the power of feedback during your rehearsal phase. Seek out honest critiques from a range of sources—not just your advisor or peers, but also individuals unfamiliar with your work. They'll give you fresh insights and help you identify the areas that need clarity from the viewpoint of a non-expert. Plus, it gets you accustomed to responding to the unexpected.

Another vital component is acclimation to your defense space. If possible, rehearse in the actual room where the defense will take place. This lets you get a feel for the environment, test out any technology you'll be using, and visualize the real event. Being familiar with the physical space can significantly reduce anxiety and improve performance.

Sure, you've read through your dissertation approximately a billion times, but can you discuss its contents conversationally? Incorporating non-scripted elements into your rehearsal will prepare you to be more adaptive and communicative rather than simply reciting a monologue. Engage with your audience during practice—ask for questions, or explain complex points in multiple ways.

When rehearsing, also consider your body language and eye contact. Your physical presentation can convey just as much as your verbal communication. Are you standing confidently? Are your gestures helping to reinforce your points, or are they distracting? Good posture and purposeful movement can heavily influence how your content is received (Poynton, 2017).

Finally, keep your goal in focus. This defense is the culmination of years of hard work. It's your opportunity to showcase not only what you know but also your passion for your field. Cultivating a mindset where you see the defense as an exciting chance to discuss your work can transform nerves into positive energy. Your enthusiasm is infectious; let it work in your favor.

Remember, the key to a successful defense isn't just potent content; it's also poise under pressure. A robust rehearsal routine sets you up for both. And as you deliver your presentation with confidence and grace, know that the tireless rehearsals have paved the way for your moment in the spotlight.

Handling Questions and Critiques

You've got your slides down pat, your presentation's rehearsed to perfection, but there's a bit more to prepping for your big day — fielding those curveball questions and critiques. This is where you transition from presenting to engaging in a dialogue with your audience, typically a panel of examiners who can throw some pretty tough pitches your way. Let's look at how you can handle this part like a pro.

First things first, get your mindset right. You're not walking into an interrogation; you're stepping into a professional discourse. Your work's going to be prodded and poked — that's a given — but remember, it's not personal. It's academia doing its thing, ensuring the cogency and vigor of intellectual inquiry. So, when questions start popping, see them as opportunities to showcase how thoroughly you've thought through your research (Wellens et al., 2021).

Start by mastering the art of the pause. Someone hits you with a gnarly question, your brain's knee-jerk reaction might be to spit out an answer faster than a cat on a hot tin roof. Resist that urge. Take a breath, collect your thoughts, and then respond. This simple pause can give your answers a veneer of consideration and control, and buys you a precious few seconds to frame a coherent response.

Echoing the question to buy more time? Smooth move. Plus, it clarifies that you've understood the question correctly. It's a win-win: you're ensuring that everyone's on the same page, and it shows thoughtful engagement. The classic "So, what you're asking is…" isn't just a stalling tactic; it's an effective communication strategy.

Got a critique that's spot on? Here's where many falter. Don't be defensive. Instead, acknowledge it. This isn't admitting defeat but showing that you can accept and engage with valid feedback. "That's an excellent point and it's something I considered during my research" can be an elegant way to segue into justification or further explanation of your choices (Harris & Carter, 2019).

But what when the critique isn't quite accurate or fair? Stay composed. Arguing or showing irritation could leave a sour taste. Instead, calmly counter with evidence, "I see where you're coming from, but let me point you to the data on page 42 that supports my approach…" This demonstrates not only your deep knowledge but also your unflappable demeanor under pressure.

Sometimes, you won't know the answer. And hey, that's okay. Academia isn't about knowing everything; it's about exploring the unknowns. Admitting, gracefully, that you don't have an answer can be powerful. "That's a great question. I didn't cover that specific angle in my research, but I'd be interested in exploring it in future work" can show intellectual humility and a readiness to learn (Kenney, 2020).

Don't forget, some questions are invitations to elaborate on parts of your research that you didn't touch upon during your presentation. Treat these as bonus rounds where you can expand on points. It could be a chance to bring up interesting tidbits that didn't make the cut for the main event but are equally as impressive.

Now, let's talk tone and language. You need to keep it professional, yet accessible. Examiners appreciate clear explanations without too much jargon or unnecessary complexity. It's about striking a balance between scholarly and understandable, staying precise without being pedantic.

And sometimes, the critiques may be less about the content and more about how you convey it. Your ability to communicate your research cogently is under the microscope too. If you stumble, that's fine, regroup and clarify. "Let me rephrase that" or "To put it another way" can guide you back on track without losing your audience's interest or patience.

It's also crucial to handle repeated questions or critiques with grace. You might feel like a broken record, but remember, each response is an opportunity to reinforce your argument or clarify a point. Keeping a positive tone helps to prevent any appearance of annoyance or dismissiveness.

Finally, practice makes everything less daunting. Do mock Q&A sessions with your peers or mentors — this can unveil weak spots in your presentation, giving you a chance to reinforce them before D-day. And who knows, one of your practice pals might just hurl a question at you that winds up coming from the examiners themselves.

Wrapping up, handling questions and critiques is as much about presentation skills as it is about your research. It's a balancing act of intellect, composure, and rhetoric. Your dissertation defense is your stage. When those spotlights come on, and the questions start flying — you've got this. You've done the research, you've prepared the material, and with a little bit of poise, you'll handle whatever comes your way.

Chapter 9:
Navigating the Defense

After countless hours of meticulous research, vigorous writing, and rounds of revision, it's showtime—the defense of your dissertation, the final boss battle in your doctoral journey. Think of it as an intellectual sparring match: not only will you showcase your work, you'll also defend it against a panel of experts who can throw some pretty unpredictable punches. This is where you need to channel your inner scholar-warrior. You've got to walk in there with an understanding of the defense process that's as thorough as your research (Targowski, 2019). Remember, confidence is your ally; it comes from knowing your dissertation inside and out, anticipating tough inquiries, and having your arsenal of data and findings primed for delivery. As you eloquently articulate your research's contribution to the field, you'll find that the interrogation isn't a hurdle but an opportunity to shine and refine. The follow-up post-defense might come with its own set of challenges (Kearns et al., 2016), but it's also your chance to prove that your work can withstand scrutiny and has wings to soar beyond the examination room. You'll leave the battlefield not just as a survivor but as a conqueror, one who's ready to take the academic world by storm. Now, let's navigate these waters, with eyes wide open and minds razor-sharp—because this is where you turn your dissertation from a piece of paper to a piece of history (Carter, 2020).

Understanding the Defense Process encompasses a crucial phase in your dissertation journey—it's where all the pieces come together, and you get to show just how much blood, sweat, and tears have gone into your research. Think of it as the grand finale of your academic performance, where you're both the director and the star. Okay, that might sound a tad dramatic, but hey, you've earned it.

Moving onto the process itself, the defense is essentially your opportunity to present your dissertation in front of a committee. This committee is usually composed of faculty members with expertise in your field, and often includes your own dissertation advisor. The composition can vary depending on your institution's guidelines, but rest assured, each one of those seated at that table is there to give your dissertation the green light... or provide you with some constructive detours.

So, what happens during a defense? Essentially, you'll be given the stage to summarize your research, walk your audience through your methodologies, present your findings, and conclude with the significance of your study. Think of it as synthesizing years of work into a nutshell—or rather, a time-constrained nutshell, as you'll have to keep an eye on the clock to ensure you cover all bases within the allotted time (usually one to two hours). My defense took almost 3 hours to complete, and I was nervous every minute of my presentation.

After your presentation, be prepared for a session of Q&A. Your committee will do a deep dive, asking questions that can range from clarifications about your methodology to the implications of your findings. It's essential to stay composed and remember that this is more of a conversation than an interrogation. Plus, it's a chance to showcase your expertise and how well you truly know your research inside and out. I was asked questions I had not anticipated, but thankfully I had memorized the majority of my study so I was able to answer most questions with ease.

Some might find this stage intimidating, and that's completely understandable. You're putting your research baby out there to be challenged! But here's the catch: It's not about defending against an attack; it's about demonstrating your critical thinking and your ability to engage with scholarly discourse.

Moreover, your defense is not just a formality—it can significantly shape the final version of your dissertation. Your committee's feedback is invaluable as it often flags areas where clarification is needed or suggests additional aspects to consider before your work joins the hallowed halls of academia (Kehoe et al., 2019). Your committee may identify weaknesses in your study. Do not let it discourage you. Listen to what they have to say and correct any deficiencies they identify.

One thing that's often overlooked in the defense process is the non-verbal communication. Your body language, eye contact, and even the way you manage your stress levels can contribute to the overall impression you make. While substance is vital, never underestimate the power of presentation.

A practical tip: engage your committee. If you can stimulate an intellectual discussion and get them nodding along, you're doing well. This engagement turns your defense into a dynamic and interactive session rather than a one-sided lecture (Snyder, 2021).

Commonly, after the questioning, you'll be asked to leave the room so the committee can deliberate on the outcome. This can be the longest wait of your life, but let's be honest, you've handled far tougher waits in your doctoral journey. When called back in, you'll be informed if you've passed, need minor revisions, major revisions, or on the very rare occasion, did not pass. The time for deliberation felt like forever. I felt like my heart stopped when my dissertation chair told me I passed. It was a very exciting moment and one that I will never forget.

Here's the comforting part: failures at this stage are infrequent. Remember, your dissertation committee has guided you this far and is typically not out to see you trip at the finish line. They want to see a solid piece of scholarly work that they can endorse and that you can be proud of (Carter, 2018).

Before walking into your defense, make sure you've read and re-read your dissertation. Yes, you wrote it, but knowing your material cold will help you respond confidently to any question thrown at you. A shaky answer just doesn't bode well, even if it's about the tiniest detail on page 84.

Once the defense is successfully behind you, and any required revisions are completed, there's the matter of submitting your final dissertation document to your institution. This submission must adhere to any specified format and be free of typos and errors. Pro tip: hire an editor if you can. A fresh pair of eyes is priceless at this stage.

Understanding the defense process means anticipating the unexpected and preparing for it with grace. Every question or comment, be it a curveball or a softball, is an opportunity to further assert the validity of your work or to consider it from a new angle.

It's not just a test of your research; it's a test of your growth as a scholar. A well-navigated defense process demonstrates not only what you have learned but how you have evolved intellectually during your doctoral odyssey. And that, dear doctoral candidate, is something worth defending with all the gusto you've got.

Presenting with Confidence

After all the months, possibly years, you've put into crafting your dissertation, you now stand on the threshold of presenting it. Imagine the scene: you enter the room, heart thudding - not with trepidation, but with the electric thrill of a challenge you're ready to meet head-on. You're about to share the fruits of your intellectual labor, and you're going to do it with panache. But what's the magic formula for presenting with the kind of confidence that captivates your audience and leaves an indelible impression? Let's dive right in.

Confidence on stage, or in this case, in your defense, may feel like something that either you have or you don't. That's a common misconception. Presenting with confidence is more of a skill than a natural-born talent, and like any skill, it can be learned, honed, and mastered (Smith et al., 2019). So, the first mental hurdle to overcome is the belief that you can't cultivate confidence. Once you're over that, it's practice, practice, and more practice.

Know your material inside out. It's not enough to have written your dissertation; you need to be able to speak about every aspect of it as though it's second nature. The deeper your understanding, the less likely you are to be thrown by unexpected questions (Johnson, 2021). Make sure you've got a solid grip on the theories, methodologies, and evidence that underpin your work. This is the groundwork that supports confidence.

Structure your presentation like a story. Everyone loves a good tale, and your defense is a unique narrative of discovery. Set the stage with a strong introduction, present the main body of your argument with enthusiasm and clear signposts, and finish with a conclusion that ties it all back together. A well-structured presentation flows and is easier for your audience to follow, which in turn boosts your confidence.

Visual aids are your allies, not crutches. Slides should enhance, not overwhelm or underwhelm your presentation. Use them to illustrate key points and maintain engagement but resist the urge to cram every detail into your slides. Your verbal narrative is the star; visual aids are the supporting cast (Brown & Green, 2020).

Pace yourself. Rushing through your presentation is a classic sign of nerves. Slow down. Breathe. Give your audience time to absorb the information, and give yourself time to find a comfortable rhythm. Pausing after critical points emphasizes their importance and shows confidence in the weight of your words.

Gestures and body language matter immensely. Open posture, moving around the space, and natural hand movements can convey enthusiasm and energy. Be animated, but not overly so. Your actions should complement your words, helping to maintain an engaging dynamic with your audience (Smith et al., 2019).

Prepare for pushback. Questions and critiques are a normal part of the defense process, not personal attacks. Anticipating potential criticisms and practicing your responses will imbue you with the confidence needed to tackle them head-on during your presentation.

Rehearse, and then rehearse some more. Do it in front of the mirror, record yourself, present to friends or peers. The more you replicate the environment of the defense, the more comfortable you'll be when the day comes (Brown & Green, 2020).

Embrace the nerves. Some degree of nervousness is natural and can even be beneficial. It keeps you alert and can enhance performance. But don't let it control you. Channel that nervous energy into your presentation by focusing on your enthusiasm for the topic rather than the sensation of anxiety.

Silence your inner critic. The voice telling you that you're not up to the task? It's not your ally. Counteract it with affirmations of your expertise and the hard work you've invested in your dissertation. You've earned the right to be where you are, sharing your research and insights.

Own your space. Whether it's a podium or the center of the room, make it yours. Your physical presence should convey authority and command attention. Practice methods that help you ground yourself in your environment, such as mindfulness or visualization techniques (Johnson, 2021).

Dress the part. It may seem trivial, but the clothing you choose can affect both your self-perception and how you're perceived by others. Opt for attire that makes you feel professional and assured, offering one less thing to worry about on the day of your defense.

Don't aim for perfection – aim for connection. Perfection is an illusion and striving for it is a surefire way to undercut your confidence. Instead, focus on connecting with your audience, conveying your passion, and delivering a clear and coherent presentation.

Finally, remember the purpose of the dissertation defense. It's not just a test; it's a conversation, a chance to discuss your work with knowledgeable peers who are interested in your research. This is the moment to celebrate your contribution to your field and to step confidently into your role as an expert.

Presenting with confidence during your dissertation defense may feel daunting, but it's within your grasp. Following these guidelines won't just help you succeed; they will elevate your presentation, making it an experience that resonates with both you and your audience. The journey to this point hasn't been easy, but it has equipped you with the knowledge and skills to stand up and share your research with conviction and poise.

Following Up Post-Defense You've just cleared a monumental hurdle—your dissertation defense. Congrats are in order, right? Absolutely. Basking in the afterglow of a successful defense is part of the process, but so is the follow-up. In this throwdown, let's jog through the essential steps you need to take after your committee has given you the nod. It's about tying loose ends, absorbing feedback, and setting the stone for future endeavors.

First off, breathe. Your post-defense journey begins with a simple yet significant act: taking the time to reflect upon and celebrate your accomplishment. But don't settle down into relaxation mode just yet. There are copies to be made, forms to be signed, and of course, feedback to mull over. If your committee has suggested revisions, as they often do, knowing exactly what's expected is key. Write it down, dissect their comments, and set up a timeline for making these changes. It's not just about ironing out the wrinkles; it's about polishing your research till it shines.

Speaking of timelines, let's chat about the importance of deadlines. Your institution will have specific guidelines on when your final dissertation must be submitted post-defense. Missing these could set you back semesters or even taint your hard work with administrative woes. It's crucial to touch base with your department's administrative assistant or the graduate school to clarify these dates and requirements.

Now, let's dig into those revisions. They might range from minor tweaks to adding a robust section to your literature review. Approach this systematically. Segregate the feedback into categories—formatting, content, theory, method... you get the gist. Prioritize what needs immediate attention based on complexity and the effort required. If your committee has asked for additional analyses, you'll need to rev up your data analysis engines once again (Johnson & Smith, 2017). These follow-up analyses can sometimes lead to new insights, augmenting the robustness of your findings.

While you're jumping through these hoops, don't let communication lag. Stay in touch with your committee. They're your allies, not gatekeepers waiting to pounce on a missed comma. Email them updates on your progress or any hurdles you're facing. Their guidance can streamline the revision process, not to mention help fend off any creeping self-doubt about your work's value (Baker et al., 2018).

Getting the nuts and bolts in order involves some bureaucracy as well. Your institution will likely have a submission protocol involving more than just handing in a paper copy. We're talking electronic repositories, author agreements, copyright considerations, and sometimes open access fees. Traverse your university's library website or get in touch with the dissertation office to understand the specifics. And make sure you keep copies of all the forms you submit—it's always smart to have a backup.

Intellectual property rights can be a murky pool to wade through, but it's an important one, especially if you're considering publishing your research (Thomas, 2021). Most institutions claim no ownership of your work, but double-check. Knowing where you stand legally regarding your research can influence future decisions about publishing or patenting.

If your program requires a 'final oral exam,' well, you're not quite out of the woods yet. Consider it a sequel to your defense, but typically with more focus on the revisions and the overall coherence of your dissertation narrative. Approach it with the same diligence—prepare, engage, and deliver.

Then there's the ultimate initiation into the brotherhood and sisterhood of scholars: getting published. Prepping your dissertation for publication is like repackaging a blockbuster movie for TV—edit, tighten, make it palatable for a wider audience. Choose a journal that aligns with your research niche, and be prepared for more feedback, this time from peer reviewers who'll have their own perspectives on your work.

But hey, let's not jump the gun. Before you dive into publication strategies, ensure your dissertation is as close to perfect as it can be. This might also be a good time to seek feedback from peers or even consider hiring a professional editor to add that final layer of polish.

Amidst all this post-defense hustle, don't forget to update your CV. It should now reflect your new status as a Ph.D. (pending any official conferral of your degree). Highlight your completed dissertation and any pending publications or presentations stemming from it. You're not just a student now; you're a researcher with cred.

Networking shouldn't take a backseat either. Engage with colleagues, attend conferences, and if possible, present your findings. These activities aren't just about showcasing your research; they're about weaving yourself into the academic fabric, threading connections that could support your career for years to come.

As for those future endeavors, start thinking about them. Whether you're leaning toward academia or have your eye on industry roles, your dissertation is a stepping stone. Use it to build on your expertise, perhaps developing subsequent research or leveraging it in a professional setting. Either way, the seeds you've sown during your doctoral journey could very well blossom into future opportunities.

And lastly, self-care. It's a tough ride, this doctoral circuit, and post-defense might feel anti-climactic. If the blues set in, remember why you started. Celebrate your grit, and don't lose sight of your achievements. Take some time for yourself—recharge, refresh, and get ready for what's next with the zeal of a scholar who's just conquered a mountain.

In essence, the follow-up post-defense isn't a mere formality; it's a critical phase that shapes the transition from student to scholar. It demands attention to detail, a proactive approach, and an understanding of the broader implications of your research (Thomas, 2021). Simply put, handle it with the same passion and precision that got you through your defense. The journey isn't over; in many ways, it's just getting started.

Chapter 10:
Maximizing the Impact of Your Research

After the often-grueling dissertation defense, don't just throw your mortarboard up and call it a day; there's a whole world out there eager to see what you've got. It's about making sure that the blood, sweat, and oh-so-many tears shed during your research journey didn't just serve as an academic rite of passage but actually toss a pebble into the pond of your field, causing ripples that matter. Translation: your research needs to get in front of eyes that will read it, respect it, and maybe even respond to it. That means honing in on the art of the publishable paper, standing tall and confident on conference stages, and not just building—but nurturing—an academic network that's robust and reciprocal. After all, a discovery that sits in a dusty library corner only really exists to the spiders that spin webs around it. By weaving together the insights you've gained from the trenches with a forward-thinking approach to disseminating your work (Thomson & Kamler, 2013), you'll not just add a line or two to your resume you'll be starting those conversations that push frontiers and flick on light bulbs in other researchers' heads. And isn't that the big-picture payoff we're all aiming for? So, don't just make it good—make it seen, make it discussed, and make it count. Penning your mark on the world in indelible ink could begin with a single citation or a handshake at a symposium, so let's get to it (Nicholas & Watkinson, 2014).

Publishing Your Findings You've crossed the Rubicon; your dissertation's ink is dry, and the time's ripe to push the boundaries of your academic enclave. Casting your pearls of wisdom into the wider sea of scholarly discourse isn't just an option—it's your duty. But let's be clear: maneuvering through the publishing landscape is like threading a needle while riding a unicycle. It's tricky, but with a little panache and a lot of perseverance, you'll do it. Here's how to escort your findings from the confines of your committee to the pages of a prestigious journal.

First things first, you're gonna want to identify the right venue. Journals are as varied as the constellations, each with its own quirks, prestige, and audience (Browman & Stergiou, 2008). Pick a journal that's in sync with your research topic and audience. No point in sending your jazz when they're all about classical.

Once you've set your sights on a journal, it's time to shape your dissertation into a manuscript. That behemoth you wrote? Pare it down. Journals love the sleek and trim—think greyhound, not mastiff. You'll need to distill your research into a concise, powerful statement that retains the meat while trimming the fat.

Before you fire off your manuscript, take a gander at the author's guidelines—each journal's got 'em, and they're as authoritative as a referee's whistle. They'll tell you everything from the required citation style to the preferred statistics flavor (American Psychological Association [APA], 2020). Follow them to the letter; deviation is the quickest path to the reject pile.

Your abstract, that tiny titan of text, is the bait on the hook. It's got to be enticing, accurate, and a distillation of your study's soul. No pressure, but it's often the deal-maker—or breaker—for would-be readers (Hartley, 2008).

Once your abstract reels them in, your introduction must lay the groundwork like a pro storyteller. Set the stage with a compelling narrative that states why your research matters, carving a path straight to your reader's curiosity nerve.

The methods section should read like a recipe a Michelin-starred chef could follow—clear, sharp, with no room for doubt. If folks can't replicate your study, they might as well be reading fiction.

Now comes the results—this is your moment, the drumroll before the reveal. Lay out your data with the precision of a watchmaker, making sure your visuals are worth a thousand words, and that your text elucidates without duplicating what's already plain to see.

But your findings aren't merely a cold recitation of data—they need to tell a story. Weave them into a narrative that links back to the big questions, the ones that keep us staring at the ceiling at 2 AM.

Don't even think of skirting the discussion section. This is where you earn your stripes, connecting dots, explaining anomalies, and humbly suggesting what your research means for the larger world. And hey, show a little spine—argue for your interpretations, but keep it gentlemanly, and acknowledge where you might have stumbled (Alley, 2018).

Let's talk about the cover letter. It's not just a formality; it's your personal ambassador. Tailor it to the journal, highlight the significance of your work but keep it from being an ego trip. Be assertive but not overbearing—think of it as a firm handshake, not a bear hug.

When you've sent your manuscript off, don't just sit back and twiddle your thumbs. Expect a volley of revisions—peer review is a dance, and you're going to be doing the tango with your reviewers. Address each comment with the gravity it deserves, but don't be a doormat; defend your work where appropriate (Rocco & Hatcher, 2011).

If you hit a roadblock and face rejection, don't throw in the towel. Rejection is just part of the game, and it doesn't mean your research isn't worthy. Take the feedback, refine your work, and pitch it to the next journal down the list. Perseverance is the name of the tune in this gig.

The day will come when you get the nod of approval, and your article is published. Don't rest on your laurels; your work's just begun. Promote your research on social media, at conferences, and in seminars. Engage with your readers and critics alike, fostering a dialogue that elevates your findings from mere words on a page to catalysts of change.

In the end, remember that publishing your dissertation is pivotal to your academic identity. It's how you contribute to the grand tapestry of knowledge, leave your mark on your discipline, and, just maybe, inspire the next soul brave enough to tread the dissertation path. It's your rite of passage—from student to scholar.

Presenting at Conferences

After pouring your heart, soul, and possibly caffeine-riddled nights into your dissertation, the time eventually comes to step out from behind the screen and into the limelight of academic forums. The symphonies of keystrokes become but a prelude to the rhythmic dance of presenting at conferences. It's the academic equivalent of the show-and-tell we once embraced as kids, but with higher stakes and a more sophisticated audience.

Consider conferences as the grand arenas where scholars from all over the cosmos convene. It's not just to show off their cerebral muscles but to engage in the communal tussle of ideas. This is your rite of passage—where your work takes a breath of fresh air, stepping out of the confines of your mind and document, and where it learns to engage critically with the thoughts and questions of others.

Getting your dissertation recognized at conferences starts with a powerful abstract. This bite-sized manifesto is your first shot at showcasing the essence of your research. It tells potential conference goers, "Hey, take a peek at what I've done." Think of it as the movie trailer for your dissertation—enticing, succinct, and leaving the audience wanting more (Figueiredo & Alarcão, 2007).

Once you've landed a spot on the conference's itinerary, creating a presentation that doesn't lull listeners into a hypnotic slumber becomes the mission. Slides, my friend, should be a palette from which your ideas burst forth in color, not a somber graveyard where bullet points go to die. Less is more. Enlist visuals that complement your oration, statistics that underscore your arguments, and just enough text to guide the conversation.

The art of verbal presentation is a beast of its own kind. You're spinning your yarn, making it relatable, maintaining eye contact—nope, not the 'staring contest' kind—and modulating your tone. It's storytelling with a purpose. The purpose is to get your audience to understand and engage with your research journey, and perhaps, find a piece of their academic soul resonating with your dissertation's melody.

Handling the question-and-answer segment is no child's play either. It's an improvised dance, and boy, you've got to tango like academia's depending on it. Think of it as an impromptu peer review. These inquiries aren't meant to trip you up but to sharpen your research's edge, helping clarify points that might have meandered through ambiguity (Harding, 2007).

Networking at these conferences is just as critical as the presentation itself. Conversations by the coffee machines or in the hallways between sessions could be serendipitous moments, leading to collaborations, future research opportunities, and maybe even a mentor or two. Keep those business cards handy and remember—every conversation could be a seed for new academic ventures.

Consider poster presentations as close cousins of the spoken presentation. It's your dissertation there, hanging out, presented graphically for the world to see. It offers a different approach, focusing on visuals and one-on-one discussions, which could be quite the change of pace for you. Nail the layout and make sure your message isn't lost in an ocean of data or a badly-chosen Comic Sans (Rowe & Ilic, 2011).

The follow-up post-conference is a gem often unmined. This isn't just a courtesy 'thank you' email to the organizers or new connections. It's about reflecting on feedback, jotting down ideas spurred by panel discussions, and perhaps plotting the course for your next academic publication. It's essentially capitalizing on the residual energy from the conference to fuel further explorations.

Think of presenting at conferences not just as a one-off event but as a chapter in your living dissertation—the one that's always open for edits, additions, and peer reviews. And maybe, just maybe, it's the part where your work ceases to be just yours and starts belonging, even if just a fragment, to the ever-expanding compendium of human knowledge.

Remember, the goal of conference presentations is not just to disseminate your findings, but to invoke discussions, to entrench your work among the scholarly threads of your discipline. It's a daunting yet exhilarating experience that can contribute tremendously to both your personal and professional growth within the academic community (Carter, Bishop & Kravits, 2007).

Presenting your dissertation at conferences is a surefire way to validate your research efforts. It's part of the great conversation of academia—a place where your work can be seen, challenged, and celebrated. It bridges the gap between the isolation of writing and the collaborative nature of scholarly work. Embrace it with open arms and see where the journey takes you.

Building an Academic Network As we step into the realm of making your research reverberate beyond the confines of your freshly bound dissertation, you can't ignore the significance of cultivating a robust academic network. Think of it as the intellectual equivalent of a thriving ecosystem, where ideas are pollinated and careers blossom.

Here, I'll walk you through the nitty-gritty of forging these essential connections, and rest assured, it's somewhat akin to an art form.

First off, understanding the value of an academic network is key. It's not just about rubbing elbows with the who's who of your field—it's a support system, a sounding board, and a source of opportunities. Guillot (2012) underscores the role of networking as a catalyst for academic and professional growth, providing access to resources and knowledge that are paramount for a burgeoning academic career.

Initiating this journey begins at your home institution. Your advisor and committee members are your foundational network. They are invaluable not only for their feedback on your work but also for introducing you to other scholars in your field. Engage with them beyond the mandatory meetings; seek their counsel, and show genuine interest in their research. Often, their connections can pave the way for your future collaborations.

Attending conferences should be on your radar next. Conferences are the melting pots of academia, where scholars from various stages and places convene. Making presentations and participating in discussions can get your name and research out there. Plus, you never know who might be sitting in the audience—potential mentors, collaborators, or even employers. Make it your mission to leave these events with more acquaintances than you came with.

Remember though, networking is not a one-time event but a continuous process. It's not enough to just exchange business cards; you have to nurture these relationships. A follow-up email expressing your appreciation for a conversation or a shared article of interest goes a long way. Think of it as tending to your professional garden—regular care leads to growth (Maxwell, 2017).

Joining academic associations can also bolster your network. These organizations often offer a plethora of resources such as newsletters, webinars, specialized groups, and even mentorship programs.

Moreover, being an active member, possibly by volunteering for committees or contributing to association publications, can shine a spotlight on your dedication and expertise (Smith, 2019).

Digital networking platforms, like LinkedIn or ResearchGate, are modern-day game changers. They allow you to connect with peers, share your work, and join scholarly discussions, all from the comfort of your desk. Properly curating your online professional presence can attract collaborators and opportunities that may have been otherwise out of reach.

Another tactic is to become a peer reviewer. While this may be a bit daunting, it's a powerful way to engage with contemporary research and get noticed by journal editors and authors alike. Moreover, it's a gesture of giving back to the academic community, which often leads to positive karma in your own scholarly pursuits.

Let's talk mentorship. Having a mentor can be transformative; they can guide you through the labyrinthine academic landscape with invaluable advice and encouragement. Don't hesitate to reach out to a scholar whose work you admire to inquire about a potential mentorship relationship. You'd be surprised how willing most are to share their wisdom (Guillot, 2012).

Contributing to your school's seminars, workshops, and colloquiums is another way to foster connections. These settings offer a more relaxed atmosphere for intellectual exchange and can lead to the establishment of collaborative relationships with faculty and students outside your immediate research circle.

But it's not all about taking; it's equally important to share your work and resources. Remember, networking is a two-way street. By offering help, insights, or even a platform for others, you create reciprocal relationships. This generosity often comes back to you tenfold. You're building a community, not just a contact list.

Writing for blogs, op-eds, or even tweeting can also expand your network. These platforms allow you to share your expertise with a broader audience and can often lead to unexpected connections with other researchers who are interested in your field of study.

Let us not forget the power of teaching. If you're in a teaching position, open your classroom (physically or virtually) to guest speakers. This not only enriches your students' experience but also strengthens your connection with colleagues and introduces you to their networks.

Diversifying your network is crucial. Don't just focus on senior academics; connecting with peers and early-career researchers can be just as rewarding. These relationships often grow and evolve as you navigate your careers together, and they can become some of the most enduring and supportive (Smith, 2019).

Lastly, be patient. Networks don't grow overnight. It takes time and effort to build meaningful relationships. Embrace the process, be genuine, and stay consistent. The seeds you plant today may bear fruit in ways you cannot yet imagine.

As you forge ahead beyond the realm of dissertations, remember that building and sustaining an academic network is integral to not just your current success, but to the enduring vitality of your career.

Chapter 11:
Time Management and Motivation

As you turn the page to time management and motivation, you're entering a realm where the tick-tock of the clock can't be ignored, and your inner fire needs kindling to keep blazing. You've got the tools from earlier chapters to build your dissertation, but here's where we fine-tune the engine. Meanwhile, your motivation, much like a temperamental beast, needs care and feeding to stay on track. Let's crack the code: managing time isn't just about listing tasks; it's recognizing that the best-laid plans are frameworks, not straitjackets. If you're going to tango with the timeline, make peace with the dance of flexibility and structure. With your goals outlined in black and white, remember that they're signposts, not chains. Setting these milestones is crucial, and science backs this up—goal setting increases success rates in nearly every field, including academia (Locke & Latham, 2002). But here's the kicker—staying motivated is tied not just to ticking off boxes but to finding intrinsic joy in every little discovery along the way. Remember that the road to dissertation bliss is paved with self-compassion, small victories, and the occasional reality check. We'll delve deep into strategies without losing sight of the human side of this scholarly quest: balancing the books with the heartbeats of your life outside the library (Sheldon & Lyubomirsky, 2006). At the end of the day, your time and motivation are the precious alchemy that'll turn research dust into doctoral gold.

Setting Realistic Goals In the thrilling quest of dissertation writing, there's a craft to setting objectives that won't make you feel like you're trying to climb Everest in flip-flops. Realistic goal setting is the linchpin between dreams and attainable aspirations. So, how do you marry ambition with achievable? Well, it's about knowing the lay of the land, being honest with yourself, and charting a course that makes sense given your unique situation.

First up, let's get a grip on what 'realistic' means in this context. 'Realistic' isn't about setting the bar so low that you could trip over it. Nor is it shooting for the stars on your first go. Instead, it's about striking a balance where your goals challenge you but don't overwhelm you to the point of paralysis (Locke & Latham, 2002).

To begin, assess your starting point. Take stock of your current skills, resources, and the time you can reasonably commit to your dissertation each week. Be clinical in this approach; overestimating what you can tackle in a day is a fast track to frustration. From this assessment, you can start setting goals that are not just wishful thinking but are grounded in the reality of your daily life.

Think about breaking your dissertation into smaller milestones or steps. Instead of viewing it as one colossal task, dissect it into digestible pieces. Have a timeline in mind, from your proposal to your final defense, and set specific, measurable goals for each phase. This technique not only makes the process less intimidating but also allows you to celebrate small victories along the way, which can be a potent motivator.

It's also crucial to set aside make-believe notions of uninterrupted days of writing and research. Let's face it, life doesn't pause just because you're working on a dissertation. Interruptions happen, so plan for them. Build buffers into your timeline and have a Plan B for when the unexpected throws a wrench in your plans. Flexibility is your friend.

When setting goals, specificity is key. "Write a chapter" is as murky as a foggy morning in San Francisco. Instead, goals like "draft the introduction section by next Friday" give you clarity and a target to aim for. Be as detailed in your planning as possible, specifying what needs to be done, when, and how you'll know it's complete (Doran, 1981).

On that note, regularly review and adjust your goals. Sometimes a goal might've seemed reasonable at the outset but turns out to be Herculean. It's ok to tweak your expectations. Rigidity only leads to broken spirits. Regular check-ins with your timeline will help you stay on track without burning out.

And hey, don't forget the importance of contingency goals. In research, not everything goes according to plan. Sometimes you have to pivot when an experiment fails, a hypothesis doesn't pan out, or a source turns out to be less relevant than you thought. Having a backup plan can save the day and keep your progress steady.

Consider also the mundane but essential aspect of goal setting: the where and how of your work. Crafting a conducive work environment is part of the goal-setting process. Whether it's ensuring you have the right software or carving out a quiet corner free from distractions, the physical and digital space in which you work will play a part in your success.

Remember to leverage the power of deadlines, too. A goal without a deadline is like a train without tracks – it's not going anywhere fast. Deadlines create a sense of urgency that can propel you forward. Just make sure your deadlines aren't too tight, or you'll be setting yourself up for stress, and let's be honest, there's enough of that to go around.

When we talk about realistic goals, we've also got to touch on self-care. Burning the midnight oil night after night might seem heroic, but it's a one-way ticket to Burnoutville. Goals should include time for rest, recreation, and relationships. After all, even the brainiest brains need downtime to work their best (Powers et al., 2018).

Teamwork makes the dream work, or so they say. Hence, don't shy away from including collaboration in your goals. Whether it's regular check-ins with your advisor or peer review sessions, connecting with others can offer fresh perspectives and encouragement. Plus, having accountability partners can keep you honest about your progress.

Lastly, recognize that good enough is good enough. In the quest for perfection, it's easy to get locked in an endless loop of revisions and doubts. Aim for excellence, not perfection. A well-done project completed is better than a perfect one forever in the making.

Setting realistic goals is all about ensuring your journey to dissertation mastery doesn't turn into a wild goose chase. It's about charting a course that's both ambitious enough to be worthwhile and achievable enough to be rewarding. Here's to setting goals that lead to triumph, not toil—a dissertation that's a testament to your skills, not a torture device. Now, let's get you set up to hit these goals, shall we?

Staying Motivated

Embarking on the dissertation journey, you've laid the foundation of your academic research, delved into the vast sea of literature, wrestled with methodologies, and dissected your data. Your scholarly quest, however, can sometimes feel like a rowing endeavor against an ebbing tide, where the shores of completion seem forever in the horizon. In these moments, the currency of motivation becomes your lifeline, preserving your passion and pushing your boat steadfastly forward.

You've heard it before, but let's engrave it in stone: maintaining motivation is not a static state of mind. It's a dynamic, pulsing endeavor. Think of your motivation as a muscle – it requires consistent nourishment and sometimes a good, hearty shake to ward off any creeping lethargy. Begin by reminding yourself of your 'why.' That original spark of curiosity that propelled you into this scholarly voyage – revisit it often (Schunk, 1991). This intrinsic anchor can rekindle the flames of engagement when the embers start to cool.

Goal setting is another catalyst for sustaining drive. The goals you set at the beginning (remember the "Setting Realistic Goals" section?) must not gather dust. Refresh them. Break down your monolithic goals into smaller, digestible tasks that you can tackle with a sense of immediacy (Locke & Latham, 2002). Each small victory accumulates momentum, fostering a sense of achievement that breeds more success. Celebrate these milestones too – indulgence in a little self-recognition goes a long way.

But here's a truth: It's not always going to be a cruise with favorable winds. Facing the doldrums is part of the process. When the slump hits, and it will, visualize your success. Picture the moment of triumph, feel the weight of that hard-earned diploma in your hands, and let this visual be the breeze that nudges your sails onward.

Now, let's talk social support systems. Human beings are not solitary islands; we thrive in connected ecosystems. Your peers, mentors, and academic colleagues can transform into a rallying crowd, cheering you toward the finish line. Establish a support group or join one if possible. When motivation wanes, a healthy exchange of experiences and encouragement from these cohorts can reframe your perspective and renew your vigor (Bandura, 1997).

On balancing the scales, it's vital to integrate work and play. When the dissertation feels all-consuming, stepping back for a 'breather' is not just advisable, it's essential. Engage in activities unrelated to research that refresh you – be it a hike, a novel, or that hobby you've placed on the back burner. Returning with a recharged battery can mean seeing your work in a new light, perhaps even prompting that eureka moment that had previously eluded you.

Don't underestimate the power of a routine either. Establishing a structured writing schedule carves out dedicated space for your dissertation work and normalizes the process. Over time, this habitual craftsmanship becomes less of a chore and more of a regular thread in the fabric of your daily life.

Digital detoxes, though seemingly a paradox in a world where research often demands technology's embrace, can provide a much-needed oasis of focus in the desert of digital distractions.

Periodically unplugging can sharpen your concentration and make space for deeper thought – a sanctuary where motivation can brew undisturbed.

An often-overlooked motivator is teaching. Explaining your research to others, whether in seminars or informal settings, can reinvigorate your enthusiasm for the topic. The process of teaching necessitates clarity and simplicity, thereby reinforcing your own understanding and connection to the research (Fiorella & Mayer, 2015).

Mining feedback also keeps motivation from running dry. Even when the critique feels less than savory, each piece of feedback is a golden nugget that can pave your scholarly path forward, solidifying your arguments, and elevating your work to unparalleled heights.

Physical health plays a role too. Don't ignore the cerebral-physical symbiosis. Regular exercise, nutritious food choices, and ample sleep are not mere bullet points in a self-care pamphlet; they are pivotal to maintaining a motivated and alert mind.

To avoid the pitfall of isolation-induced demotivation, participate in scholarly communities. Online forums, academic conferences, or local meet-ups can serve as your intellectual tribe, providing a sense of belonging, shared purpose, and collective energy.

Furthermore, diversifying your workflow can combat the stagnation that monotony breeds. Switch between writing, reading, and data analysis to keep your brain gymnastically engaged with the myriad dimensions of your dissertation.

Lastly, make room for reflection. Periodically stepping back to assess your progress, celebrate your growth, and recalibrate your direction is critical. These tranquil moments of introspection can remind you of the ground covered and the peaks yet to conquer.

In conclusion, staying motivated requires a multifaceted approach: nurturing your intrinsic interests, setting and revisiting goals, visualizing success, leaning on your support network, harmonizing work with leisure, adhering to routine, occasionally disconnecting from the digital world, teaching, drawing wisdom from feedback, maintaining physical health, immersing in scholarly communities, diversifying tasks, and indulging in reflective practice. Understand that motivation is not merely found—it is fostered, cajoled, and sometimes wheedled into existence. Your dissertation journey is uniquely yours, and how you motivate yourself to travel this road will define not only your experience but also the caliber of your scholarly work.

Balancing Life and Research

You've unstacked shelves of dense literature, scrutinized methodologies, and you're adept at wrangling with data. Now, let's talk about juggling—the relentless act of keeping your research, personal life, and potentially a job, all spinning in the air without dropping the ball. Here's the kicker: it's more art than science.

Finding harmony between life and research demands a finesse that can feel akin to walking a tightrope. It's a balancing act that has no one-size-fits-all solution, but requires constant adjustments to steady yourself on the wire. Acknowledge this: your well-being is pivotal to your research success. Neglect it, and the entire endeavor can come crashing down. My motto has always been family first. Remember to take time for your family and yourself.

First, let's dissect the myth of the "ideal" researcher—the one who toils day and night with no need for downtime. That's fantasy. Everybody needs a respite. If you continuously push without a break, you're setting yourself up for burnout (Maslach & Leiter, 2016). Balance isn't a luxury; it helps maintain a sustainable pace. It's about efficiency, not the number of hours clocked in. Work smarter, not harder.

Think of your time as a pie chart. It shouldn't be a monolithic block of research. Slice that pie up. Dedicate time for family, friends, exercise, hobbies, and rest. Yes, your dissertation is important, but so is your son's soccer game, your best friend's wedding, and your mental health. Learn to say no, or better yet, decide what you must say yes to—then prioritize.

Now, how about syncing up with your body's rhythm? Are you a night owl or an early bird? Tailor your schedule to when your intellectual engine runs at its peak. You'll be more productive during those golden hours, leaving space for the rest of your life in the off-peak times (Circadian rhythms research).

Then there's the boogeyman of procrastination. It haunts everyone, whispering sweet somethings about later being a fine time to get things done. Here's an antidote: break down your monstrous tasks into bite-sized pieces. When a task seems manageable, it's less likely to be shunted off into the future (Pychyl & Flett, 2012).

Communication is a crucial gear in your balance machine. Keep your advisor and peers in the loop about your schedule constraints. They can't support you if they don't know what you're up against. And you never know—they might have been in your shoes before and could offer some sage advice or flexibility.

Here's a truth bomb: guilt can be a relentless side-effect of seeking balance. You might feel guilty for not working on your dissertation during a family outing or feel bad for spending time in the lab when you think you should be at home. Accept that these feelings are normal, but don't let them govern you. Remember, taking care of your relationships and yourself is part of being a well-rounded researcher.

Sleep—don't skimp on it. You might think burning the midnight oil is a badge of honor, but it's more like shooting yourself in the foot. Sleep deprivation messes with your cognitive functions, creativity, and even ethical decision-making (Barnes et al., 2011). A rested brain is a more effective brain.

Also, consider the power of routines. They free up mental bandwidth by making certain behaviors automatic, providing structured flexibility (Wood & Rünger, 2016). Your morning could include exercise, then research, followed by personal time in the evening. This framework can help you transition between different areas of life smoothly.

Exercise: it's not just for the body, but for the brain too. Physical activity can improve mood, reduce stress, and even enhance cognitive functions—all of which are your allies in research (Ratey, 2008). Consider it a three-pronged power-up for your life and academic pursuits.

Let's talk tech: apps and tools designed for time management can be life-savers. They can help you track your work and breaks, reminding you when to switch gears. But remember, technology is a tool, not a tyrant. Customize it to serve you, not to dictate your day.

Lastly, embrace flexibility. Life is unpredictable. Sometimes, despite your best plans, things will go awry—a family emergency, a health issue, or simply a slump in motivation. Being rigid in your plans will only lead to frustration. Adapt, adjust, and accept that some days won't go according to script.

In conclusion, balancing life and research is about being self-aware, strategic with your time, and forgiving toward yourself when things don't go perfectly. Treat balance as another research project. Experiment, observe, and tweak your approach until you find what works best for you. Remember that your dissertation is just a part of your life, not the entirety of it.

Chapter 12:
Preparing for Post-Dissertation Opportunities

Having navigated the tumult of research and emerged victorious with a polished dissertation, you're now standing on the precipice of what comes next. But, hold your horses—it's not time to take the plunge without a game plan. This chapter is your strategic guide to seizing post-dissertation opportunities with both hands. Let's dive into piecing together your next moves, ensuring your transition from doctoral candidate to seasoned professional or academic is as smooth as peanut butter. First up, you gotta think about your career trajectory. Are you gunning for a tenure track, itching to impart wisdom to the next wave of bright minds, or are you more enticed by the siren call of industry, where practical application of your research awaits? And don't forget, learning's a lifelong gig—this chapter's got the goods on keeping your brain buff through continuous development. You're not just closing a chapter of academic rigor; you're flipping the page to a fresh chapter brimming with potential. It's about charting a course that capitalizes on the skills you've honed, the knowledge you've amassed, and the network you've woven—a roadmap for creating waves in your chosen field.

Academic Career Paths

Embarking on an academic career after that final flourish of your doctoral cap and gown is quite the adventure, one that offers a cornucopia of paths, each with their unique sets of challenges and rewards. Understanding what lies ahead can help you tailor your dissertation journey to fit the future role you're aiming for. So let's delve into what it really means to pursue a career in academia, post-dissertation.

First up, the quintessential goal for many: becoming a tenure-track professor. This is the golden ticket of academic careers for some, signifying a permanent spot in the hallowed halls of a university. To get there, you'll generally kick things off as an assistant professor, where publishing research and teaching become your bread and butter. Prove your mettle during this period, usually around six years, and you might just be granted tenure – a status which offers job security and the academic freedom to research to your heart's content.

However, before you even start dreaming of tenure, there's a step often encountered fresh out of a PhD program: the postdoctoral fellowship. This is your chance to deepen your research expertise, often with a bit more freedom than during your doctoral studies. It's a time for expanding your publication list, working alongside seasoned researchers, and honing in on your niche (Bellas, 1999).

Aside from the traditional laurels of academia, another occupation that's increasingly gaining traction is that of a research scientist, often within a university but sometimes with government agencies or private research institutes. Here, your day-to-day is immersed in exploration and experimentation, less in teaching. The emphasis is on producing high-caliber research and contributing to the body of knowledge in your field (Stephan, 2012).

Teaching-focused roles are also prevalent, and one might opt for positions such as a lecturer or teaching professor. These roles prioritize imparting knowledge and supporting the academic growth of students rather than conducting research. A knack for compelling storytelling and an ability to demystify complex concepts go a long way here.

For those who love the nexus of academia and administration, roles such as department chairs or deans might be the perfect fit. In these positions, you could influence educational policies, oversee faculty, and manage budgets while still keeping a hand in teaching or research activities.

Now, if you can't resist the call of juggling both academia and industry, consider being a consultant or an entrepreneur. Use your analytical prowess to solve real-world problems or even start your own venture — this route offers opportunities to apply research in tangible, impactful ways.

Don't forget the unconventional yet vital role of academic librarianship, where managing information resources, assisting with research, and teaching information literacy skills make up your mission. It's an ideal job for those who are organized, digitally savvy, and passionate about supporting the academic community's quest for knowledge.

Academic publishing is a sector for those enamored with the written word and the dissemination of knowledge. Roles include editing, peer reviewing, and curating scholarly content. Here, your sharp eye for detail and understanding of academic rigor are key (Cronin, 2005).

Of course, let's not sideline the importance of mentorship roles. Senior academics often serve as mentors, offering guidance, support, and helping shape the future generation of researchers.

But let's be real, the trajectory isn't always linear. Be prepared for zigzags and hurdles. Funding cuts, institutional changes, and the competitive nature of academia mean that resilience, perseverance, and a bit of savvy navigation are required. It's about finding that sweet spot between what you love, what you're great at, and what will keep the lights on.

Remember, too, the power of networking. Building a robust academic network can open doors to collaborations, job opportunities, and the sharing of ideas. Your dissertation's acknowledgment section shouldn't be the last time you thank your peers and mentors!

In essence, your PhD journey is akin to carving your own wand in the wizarding world of academia. It's personalized, intricate, and packed with potential for magic. Post-dissertation, you wield that wand with more confidence, ready to make your mark in whichever realm of academia or beyond that beckons most sweetly to your scholarly soul.

Chunking this down, academic career paths are vast and varied. The key takeaway: assess what excites you most about academia, align your skills and interests, and navigate towards roles that fulfill your intellectual and personal goals. And remember, the journey itself transforms you, gifting you with knowledge, insights, and experiences that will illuminate whichever path you choose.

Take it one step at a time. Start by maximizing the impact of your dissertation research, publish relentlessly, engage in academic conversations, and most importantly, be open to growth and learning. An academic career is as much a vocation as it is a profession, and your doctoral journey is just the beginning.

So, as you wrap up those final pages of your dissertation, let your mind wander to the possibilities that lie ahead. The career paths within academia are as diverse as the disciplines they encompass, giving you the freedom to carve out a niche that's truly your own.

Industry Opportunities Diving into the depths of your dissertation, it's easy to tunnel-vision on the academic accolades awaiting at the end of this colossal climb. Yet, that's only a slice of the pie. Your brainchild - the dissertation - is more than just fodder for the scholarly crowd; it's a passport to a universe of industry possibilities. Sure, donning the robe and the honor of 'Dr.' is the dream, but let's talk shop—the industry kind.

Now, don't get me wrong. Academia is a noble pursuit, but outside its ivory towers lies a dynamic world where your research can have real-world impact. Industries are thirsty for know-how that cuts to the chase, solves problems, and innovates—or in your case, research that translates to the bottom line. Analyzing your dissertation through an industry lens can lead to a trove of opportunities, from consultancy gigs to R&D think tanks.

Think about it. Organizations are on the hunt for individuals who can back up their intuition with hard evidence and those who can sift through data to find the gold nuggets of insight. Your scholarly endeavors have armed you with a toolkit that's ripe for the plucking in sectors hungry for data-driven decision-making and thought leadership. It's not just about the numbers; it's about weaving a narrative that resonates with stakeholders.

You're crafting an original piece of work, a research delicacy that's both a credential and testament to your tenacity. It's not just the content that's valuable, though that's a significant part of it. The diligence, the analytical acumen, the hours you've committed—they all add up to a compelling argument for why an industry might want to snatch you up. They're itching for that blend of grit and intellect; someone who won't buckle under pressure.

Expose your dissertation to the industry, and you open doors to becoming the go-to expert in your field. For instance, if your research is in educational technology, EdTech startups could be drooling over your insights. Every paragraph you sweat over might contain the kernel of innovation that leads to the next great learning platform. Let's not undersell it; your findings could revolutionize how society learns and interacts with information.

Now, let's draw back the curtain on funding streams. Embarking on your dissertation may have been an exercise in financial tightrope walking, but in the business hemisphere, there's a rainbow's pot of gold. Corporations invest heftily in R&D, and they're eager for new perspectives. Align your research with industry needs, and you might just find your dissertation bankrolled by the very companies who stand to benefit from it.

Collaborations and networking are not mere buzzwords in this scenario; they're your bread and butter. Forge relationships with industry professionals keen on academic partnerships, and you'll pinpoint opportunities that were invisible from the confines of the campus coffee shop. Remember, your dissertation topic can turn heads in conference rooms just as easily as in lecture halls.

Your defense isn't merely a nod of approval from a panel of professors. It's proof that you've got the chops to argue, to defend, to innovate. These transferable skills are in high demand in the industry, where pitching ideas and thinking on your feet are all in a day's work. That gauntlet you ran during your defense? It was a trial by fire, preparing you for high-stakes meetings with clients or executives.

Now, imagine your dissertation as a polished pebble tossed into the industry pond, creating ripples that extend beyond what you initially thought possible. It might not just influence policies and practices, but also be the springboard for new technology or processes that transform an entire sector. The tech scheme you've outlined could be the pith of a new software system or a patent that catapults you into the entrepreneurial arena.

Don't overlook the entrepreneurial potential here. Spin-offs and startups are birthed from dissertations that dared to defy the status quo. Maybe you've unearthed a niche, a way to better society that the market hasn't even sniffed out yet. Your research desk could be the drawing board for a venture that disrupts markets and lives on long after the final word of your dissertation is penned.

Your appetite for research need not end with academia's stamp of approval. The corporate realm may offer resources and opportunities to continue your inquiries but on a scale that could amplify your reach and magnify the impact of your findings. Your dissertation may become the cornerstone of an industry-wide reference or a product that becomes household by name.

And then there's the potential for policy impact. Yes, the drudgery of line edits and data sets might feel worlds away from the halls of power, but governments and agencies hunger for solid research to base regulations on. Your academic rigor could very well lay the groundwork for legislative changes or social campaigns that reshape the fabric of communities.

The translation of your research into practical solutions for industry challenges is like decoding an ancient script. It's revealing the sacred to the secular—making the esoteric accessible and applicable. In the process, you're not just proving theories, but proving your worth in a market that respects and requires the analytical prowess you possess.

Last by not least, let's tackle professional development. The dissertation journey hones skills that are gold dust in the industry: critical thinking, complex problem solving, and clear communication. Your capability to juggle multiple tasks, from data crunching to theory development, preps you for project management and leadership roles in any field.

All said and done, your dissertation could be more than a lofty academic exercise. It's a ladder to untold industry vistas where your scholarly skills are not just a display of intellectual brawn but a valued currency that can push the boundaries of what's possible within the corporate sphere. So, let those chapters shape not just your CV, but also the trajectory of industries poised for the innovation and expertise that only you can provide.

Lifelong Learning and Development

After the marathon of your dissertation, you might imagine your scholarly pursuits dwindling on the horizon. Think again. The reality is, that achievement unlocks a lifelong learning and development path diversely rich and vibrantly endless. It's like realizing you've been swimming in the pond when there's an ocean out there. Just by engaging with your research, you've primed the pump for an unending flow of knowledge and skill accumulation. So, let's dive into how you can keep that current flowing post-dissertation.

Your research has been a deeply intense learning experience. It's important to understand that learning doesn't cease upon graduation; it merely evolves. Developing a mindset geared towards continuous education can boost your career, enhance your expertise, and enrich personal growth (Smith & Robertson, 2017). Engaging in new research, attending workshops, and furthering your education through courses or certificates are practical ways to maintain intellectual curiosity and professional relevance.

Similarly, your participation in scholarly communities and networks is not just for the here and now. It's a long-term investment. These relationships often sprout opportunities for collaboration, joint research projects, or even mentorship roles. Remember, you've now moved into the realm of a scholar practitioner, and expanding your network is crucial for keeping abreast of the latest trends and breakthroughs in your field.

Think also about teaching. Whether it's a formal setting at a university or an informal workshop, sharing your knowledge is both a service to others and a boon for your own understanding. Teaching forces you to articulate concepts clearly and often leads to deeper insights about your own research. Plus, the questions students raise can spark new avenues of inquiry (Wells, 2019).

Reflecting on your methodology and results can germinate ideas for further study. A doctoral dissertation is often just an elaborate pilot study in the grand scheme of things. Many doctoral graduates find that their dissertation is just the starting point for a wider program of research. What questions were left unanswered? What paths were left unexplored? These reflections can help you chart a course for future investigations.

Post-dissertation, consider the importance of publications in academic journals. By regularly submitting your work for publication you contribute to the discourse in your field and establish yourself as an authority (Doe et al., 2021). Not every submission will be a home run, but the feedback received can refine your thinking and writing. This iterative process is a cornerstone of academic development.

It's also imperative to consider the role of interdisciplinary learning. The world's complexities increasingly demand knowledge beyond the narrow confines of single disciplines. Reaching out into adjacent areas of study can not only provide fresh perspectives on your own research but can also lead to innovative partnerships and approaches. Interdisciplinary collaboration can open doors to new fields of inquiry and methods that can profoundly influence your work.

Your development also has a digital dimension in this era. Ensuring that you are proficient with the latest software and platforms in your field can make a significant difference. From data analysis tools to digital collaboration platforms, your ability to harness technology can streamline your research, enhance your productivity, and expand your methodological toolkit.

A critical component often overlooked in the learning process is reflection. Taking regular stock of your experiences, successes, and failures, and then using that analysis to inform future decisions, is indispensable for personal and professional growth. Reflective practice can lead to greater resilience and adaptability, traits that are critical for navigating the unpredictable waters of a research career.

You might also consider writing a book or developing a course based on your dissertation research. By doing so, you extend the reach of your work and solidify your expertise. Moreover, it's a chance to clarify your thoughts, structure your knowledge, and create a legacy that can guide others in their journey.

And let's not discount the power of consultation. Offering your expertise as a consultant can not only be financially rewarding but can also present you with real-world problems that can inform your academic work. Consulting can bridge the gap between theory and practice, allowing for a circular flow of knowledge that enriches both.

Entering the blogging or podcasting arena can also serve as learning and development platforms. By discussing your research with a broader audience, you refine your capacity to communicate complex ideas in an accessible manner. This not only hones your communication skills but also enhances your visibility as an expert in your field.

An effective way to stay in the loop with academic developments is to serve on editorial boards or review panels. Such roles not only allow you to contribute to the quality of publications in your field but also give you early access to cutting-edge research and the opportunity to engage with other scholars in peer review processes.

Remember, your doctoral degree is a foundation from which your personal and professional life can grow in immeasurable ways. It's the beginning of a journey that continually shapes you as a scholar. With every step you take in furthering your education and contributing back to your field, you refine your skills, enhance your career prospects, and, perhaps most importantly, fulfill your potential as a lifelong learner.

Chapter 13:
The Journey Beyond

The scent of freshly printed pages filled the air, signaling not an end but a gateway to new beginnings. You've navigated the winding roads of research questions, methodology, and data analysis. You've triumphed over the gauntlet of peer reviews and the adrenaline-fueled theater of dissertation defenses. Your academic odyssey has sculpted you into not just a scholar, but a sagacious guide equipped for the unknown terrain that lies beyond the venerated halls of academia.

As you stand on this threshold, clutching the tome of your endeavors, it's easy to be ensnared by a web of what-ifs and where-to-nexts. Don't fret. The graduate journey you've undertaken has armed you with a quiver of skills that are transferrable and invaluable in the wilds of any career pathway you choose.

The knowledge you've harvested is ripe for sharing. Think back to the inception of your study—your findings weren't just an answer to your question but a lantern for others in the shadow of their inquiries. Publishing your work isn't merely a tip of the hat to personal success; it's your contribution to the rich tapestry of collective human understanding (Byrne, 2019).

And let's not understate the soft skills you've accrued along the way. The relentless hours of crafting arguments and the relentless pursuit of insight have honed your thinking into something keen and critical. These are the swords you bear into battles of intellect and strategy, be they in academic skirmishes or the broader forums of public discourse.

Use this acumen to fuel your presentations at conferences, where new minds will grapple with your work. Attend. Speak. Debate. Each interaction is a brick laid in the edifice of your professional network—a structure that should be as robust as your thesis (Hamilton & McMillan, 2021).

While some will etch their names into the stones of academia, others will find paths in industry that are equally as rewarding. Don't view these two realms as mutually exclusive; the bridge between theory and practice is traversed by many who find harmonies in their dissonance.

What of the might-have-beens, the paths not taken, the questions unasked? Every study has its boundaries, its limitations. Yet these aren't failures but seeds—each capable of growing into its own journey of inquiry. Reflection on what you didn't or couldn't explore provides a roadmap for those who follow in your footsteps, or perhaps for your future investigations.

Education isn't a terminus, but a perpetual motion machine. The rigor of doctoral studies fosters a mindset where learning never ceases. Engage with this state of constant curiosity. Lean into the discomfort of not knowing, for it is the crucible where new knowledge is formed.

Beyond the shadow of the cap and gown, the journey is far from over. It continues with mentoring others, shaping the scholars who will march to the rhythm of keystrokes on keyboards long after you've laid your pen down. Passing the torch isn't a relinquishing of duty but the fulfilling of a role as vital as that of the researcher.

Your toolkit is brimming with the essentials for time management—a skill arguably as crucial outside the academic sphere as within it. As you map out your future, remember the balance you sought between life and research. A fulfilled life can fuel successful work, and neither needs to be sacrificed for the other (Gardner et al., 2022).

For some, the allure of the lecture halls and lab benches will beckon them back. Teaching and research positions within the academy offer the chance to delve deeper, to answer the calls of the unanswered questions. For those who yearn for this avenue, remember the peaks and pits of your own journey, and strive to smooth the path for those in your charge.

Yet for others, the insights gained through research will call them to industry shores. There, challenges await that require the rigor of a researcher's eye but within the framework of practical application. Don't underestimate the transformative power you wield; your abilities to analyze, synthesize, and catalyze change are sought after beyond the ivy-clad walls.

Wherever your journey takes you, commitment to lifelong learning ensures the voyage remains vibrant and that your scholarly muscles never atrophy from disuse. Your doctoral journey has prepped you to adopt new technologies, assimilate into shifting job landscapes, and contribute meaning in myriad unforeseen ways.

Remember, the journey beyond is not just about career trajectories and scholarly contributions. It's also about the introspective odyssey that accompanies years of dedicated study. You've cultivated resilience, nurtured patience, and learned the intricate dance of discipline and creativity. Carry these inner triumphs forward—they are your silent companions as you navigate the path ahead.

And so, as you cross the bridge that spans from the comfort of known scholarly pursuits to the vast landscape of possibility, walk with confidence. You're no longer just a passenger on this academic vessel. You're now the captain, steering through uncharted waters with the stars of knowledge to guide you. Bon voyage!

Appendix A:
Dissertation Checklist

Embarking on your dissertation journey is a bit like setting out on an epic quest. You'll need patience, persistence, and a detailed map to guide you through the wilds of academic research. Consider this checklist as your compass, ensuring you don't miss the crucial stops along the path to dissertation success.

Getting Started

Define your research question (*Chapter 1*).

Ensure all necessary ethics approvals are in place (*Chapter 1*).

Compile a preliminary bibliography of relevant literature (*Chapter 2*).

Literature Review

Conduct a comprehensive literature search (*Chapter 2*).

Read and take notes, synthesizing key points (*Chapter 2*).

Organize literature into themes or categories (*Chapter 2*).

Methodology Design

Choose between qualitative or quantitative methods (Chapter 3).

Outline your research design, including sampling and procedures (Chapter 3).

Determine which data collection techniques to employ (Chapter 3).

Data Collection and Analysis

Collect your data systematically (*Chapter 3*).

Analyse your data, employing appropriate software tools (*Chapter 4*).

Interpret the results with academic integrity (*Chapter 4*).

Writing and Revision

Structure your dissertation, following your program's guidelines (*Chapter 5*).

Maintain a scholarly tone and writing style throughout (*Chapter 5*).

Overcome writer's block with proven strategies (*Chapter 5*).

Peer Review and Defense Preparation

Submit your dissertation for peer review (*Chapter 6*).

Revise your dissertation based on feedback (*Chapter 6*).

Prepare your defense presentation and anticipate critiques (*Chapter 8*).

The Final Stretch

Perfect your presentation slides and rehearse your defense (*Chapter 8*).

Confidently present and defend your dissertation (*Chapter 9*).

Follow up on any post-defense revisions or requirements (*Chapter 9*).

Make sure you've ticked all the boxes here. However, remember, flexibility is the name of the game. Sometimes, you need to adapt your strategy as new challenges emerge. Don't get so wedded to the plan that you lose sight of the end goal - getting that research out there and making a splash!

Don't forget; this checklist serves as a guide, not gospel. Your own journey may have additional steps, or you might blaze through some parts faster than others. Stay in tune with the beat of your own drum, and when necessary, consult with your advisor – they're like your sherpa on this mountain climb.

By ensuring each of these elements is adequately addressed, you position yourself well for the ascent to the dissertation summit. Keep climbing; the view from the top is worth every step.

Appendix B:
Sample Dissertation Timeline

Embarking on a dissertation can feel like trying to navigate through a thick fog with a dim flashlight—you know there's a path, but darn if it isn't hard to see the whole trail from where you're standing. That's why it's essential to create a timeline, a lighthouse of sorts, to shine a light on the key milestones ahead and keep your steps steady as you march onward to your academic triumph.

Year 1

Month 1-3: Begin with the formality of coursework, letting the seeds of your research question germinate as you delve deeper into your field.

Month 4-6: Start narrowing down topics, casting your net wide in the literature, and identifying gaps that your study could fill. Preliminary discussions with potential advisors should also be in full swing.

Month 7-9: Zero in on your research question (Locke et al., 2009). It's like finding the perfect puzzle piece that clicks in just right—you'll know when you've got it.

Month 10-12: Round out your literature review. Know those sources like you know the back of your hand (or even better, since let's be honest, who really studies the back of their hand?).

Year 2

Month 1-3: Finalize your methodology—qualitative, quantitative, or, for those who like to mix and mingle, a bit of both (Creswell & Creswell, 2017).

Month 4-6: Apply for ethical approvals, if needed. The bureaucracy may sometimes grind slower than you'd like, but it's all part of the process.

Month 7-9: Begin data collection. It's like a treasure hunt where the treasure is data and glory (ok, mostly just data).

Month 10-12: Continue collecting data. If you're feeling stuck, remember, slow and steady data collection can win this academic race.

Year 3

Month 1-3: Start analyzing your data. This phase is where the magic starts to happen, or at least where you start to seriously doubt all your life choices (which is normal, by the way).

Month 4-6: Complete your data analysis and begin drafting the results section. This is like trying to tell the story of what you've found without letting the data run off on tangents.

Month 7-9: Write your discussion section, linking the dots between your results and the big picture of your field.

Month 10-12: Finalize your full draft and start the editing process. Think of it as carving a rough sculpture into David—you're chipping away at the block to reveal the masterpiece within.

Year 4

Month 1-3: Undergo the peer review process and revise extensively. It's about honing your work until it's so sharp it could cut glass (figuratively speaking, of course) (Belcher, 2019).

Month 4-6: Defend that dissertation. It's showtime! You've prepared for this; just remember to breathe.

Month 7-9: Address any post-defense revisions and prepare the final manuscript for submission. You're in the home stretch now.

Month 10-12: Submit your dissertation and proceed to celebrate—responsibly, of course. The feeling of accomplishment will be your best dessert.

Remember, life can throw all sorts of curveballs, so treat this timeline as a guide, not gospel. It's meant to keep you on track, but it's not a life sentence. The flexibility to pivot and adapt can't be overstated—you're in it for the finish, not just the sprint.

Appendix C:
Resources and Further Reading

You've plowed through the chapters, soaked up oodles of advice, and are now poised at the final ledge before soaring into the great academic yonder. This is where you roll up your sleeves and dig into the wealth of resources awaiting you. Once you step out the door, you don't want to feel like you're jumping without a parachute, right? So here's your gear - a collection to fuel that mind of yours and keep those synapses firing on all cylinders.

Books and E-Books

Dissertations and theses can't write themselves, but reading around the subject area never hurt anyone – in fact, it might just be your golden ticket. Make sure to have a gander at these:

The Dissertation Warrior: Consider this your personal trainer for the dissertation marathon. It's got insights, strategies, and pep talks to keep you keyed up and on track.

Writing Your Dissertation in Fifteen Minutes a Day: Don't let the title mislead you; it's about creating habits that foster consistent progress, and goodness knows we could all use more of that.

The Craft of Research: This is the Grand Poobah of research books. You can't go wrong with a classic, and this one has been steering students right for years.

Academic Journals

Peering through journal articles isn't quite as drab as it sounds - it's like panning for gold. These scholarly publications can be your best buddies:

Journal of Scholarly Publishing: It gets meta, talking about publishing while you're about to get something publishable. Good for insights on the industry and best practices.

Educational Researcher: Grab this for the latest studies and musings on education – perfect for keeping tabs on contemporary happenings (American Educational Research Association, 2020).

The Journal of Higher Education: For eyeballing the broader landscape of higher ed and understanding where your research could fit in the grander scheme.

Online Resources

We're not talking about mindlessly scrolling through social media here - these online resources are digital goldmines:

Google Scholar: It's like Google's more sophisticated cousin, and a lifesaver for finding scholarly articles, books, and papers. I utilized this resource more than my university's online library.

ResearchGate: Snazzy for connecting with other researchers and getting access to papers you might otherwise have missed. It's networking with a scholarly twist.

ORCID: As you carve out your academic persona, getting an ORCID iD helps keep all your research work neatly under one roof online - very handy for citations and keeping your work attributed to you.

Writing and Citation Tools

Don't let references get your goat or formatting flummox you – these tools will keep everything neat and tidy:

EndNote: It's like the Swiss Army knife for writing large documents like dissertations. One tool, many purposes – from managing references to formatting bibliographies.

Zotero: A free tool that's brilliant for gathering, organizing, citing, and sharing research. Plus, its community is always there if you get stuck (Roy Rosenzweig Center for History and New Media, n.d.). This program was a lifesaver during my program.

Grammarly: Because everyone needs a grammar cop – this one's automated and doesn't take coffee breaks.

Recite: This site is fantastic for checking your dissertation for errors with citations. I used this site with every iteration of my dissertation.

This is by no means an exhaustive list, but it's a sturdy launching pad. The journey through your dissertation is a hefty challenge, but you've got a whole arsenal of resources at your fingertips. Always remember to evaluate the quality and relevance of your resources to your specific dissertation - after all, you're the expert in making your research shine.

References

APA. (2020). Publication manual of the American Psychological Association (7th ed.). American Psychological Association.

Adams, J., & Lawrence, E. (2019). Research Methods, Statistics, and Applications. SAGE Publications.

Aitchison, C., Kamler, B., & Lee, A. (2010). Publishing Pedagogies for the Doctorate and Beyond. Routledge.

Alley, M. (2018). The craft of scientific writing (4th ed.). Springer.

Alley, M., & Neeley, K. A. (2005). Rethinking the design of presentation slides: A case for sentence headlines and visual evidence. Technical Communication, 52(4), 417-426.

American Educational Research Association. (2020). Educational Researcher.

American Psychological Association. (2020). Publication manual of the American Psychological Association (7th ed.). American Psychological Association.

Angrosino, M. V., & Rosenberg, J. (2011). Observations on Observation: Continuities and Challenges. In N. Denzin & Y. Lincoln (Eds.), The Sage Handbook of Qualitative Research (4th ed., pp. 467-478). Sage Publications.

Animal Welfare Act, 7 U.S.C. § 2131 et seq. (1966).

Association for Psychological Science. (2019). Mindfulness meditation for anxiety, depression. Psychological Science Agenda.

https://www.psychologicalscience.org/observer/mindfulness-meditati
on-for-anxiety-depression

Baker, S., Thompson, K., & Lee, M. Y. (2018). The academic afterlife:
Post-defense practices and considerations for a successful transition.
Graduate Education Journal, 15(3), 87-99.

Bandura, A. (1997). Self-efficacy: The exercise of control. W. H.
Freeman.

Barnes, C. M., Schaubroeck, J., Huth, M., & Ghumman, S. (2011).
Lack of sleep and unethical conduct. Organizational Behavior and
Human Decision Processes, 115(2), 169-180.

Belcher, W. L. (2019). Writing your journal article in twelve weeks: A
guide to academic publishing success (2nd ed.). University of Chicago
Press.

Bellas, M. L. (1999). Emotional Labor in Academia: The Case of
Professors. Annals of the American Academy of Political and Social
Science, 561(1), 96-110.

Boell, S. K., & Cecez-Kecmanovic, D. (2015). On being 'systematic' in
literature reviews. Journal of Information Technology, 30(2), 161-173.

Boice, R. (1994). How writers journey to comfort and fluency: A
psychological adventure. Westport, CT: Praeger.

Bolker, J. (1998). Writing Your Dissertation in Fifteen Minutes a Day:
A Guide to Starting, Revising, and Finishing Your Doctoral Thesis.
Henry Holt and Company.

Boote, D. N., & Beile, P. (2005). Scholars before researchers: On the
centrality of the dissertation literature review in research preparation.
Educational Researcher, 34(6), 3-15.

Booth, W. C., Colomb, G. G., & Williams, J. M. (2008). The Craft of
Research (3rd ed.). University of Chicago Press.

Booth, W. C., Colomb, G. G., & Williams, J. M. (2008). The Craft of Research. University of Chicago Press.

Booth, W. C., Colomb, G. G., & Williams, J. M. (2016). The Craft of Research (4th ed.). University of Chicago Press.

Borrego, M., & Newswander, L. K. (2010). Definitions of interdisciplinary research: Toward graduate-level interdisciplinary learning outcomes. Review of Higher Education, 34(1), 61-84.

Bowen, W. G., & Rudenstine, N. L. (2020). In Pursuit of the PhD. Princeton University Press.

Boyd, D., & Crawford, K. (2012). Critical questions for Big Data: Provocations for a cultural, technological, and scholarly phenomenon. Information, Communication & Society, 15(5), 662-679.

Bramer, W. M., Rethlefsen, M. L., Kleijnen, J., & Franco, O. H. (2017). Optimal database combinations for literature searches in systematic reviews: A prospective exploratory study. Systematic Reviews, 6(1), 245.

Browman, H. I., & Stergiou, K. I. (2008). Factors and indices are one thing, deciding who is scholarly, why they are scholarly, and the relative value of their scholarship is something else entirely. Ethics in Science and Environmental Politics, 8(1), 1-3.

Brown, G., & Green, T. (2020). The Art of Presentation: Your Competitive Edge. Presentation Dynamics.

Bryman, A. (2016). Social Research Methods. Oxford University Press.

Bryman, A. (2016). Social research methods. Oxford university press.

Byrne, J. (2019). Academic and scientific publishing: Strategies for increasing visibility and dissemination of scholarly work. Journal of Scholarly Publishing, 50(3), 123-134.

Carter, S. (2018). Conquering Your Dissertation: Advice from the Trenches. University Press of Academia.

Carter, S. (2020). The dissertation difference. Journal of Graduate Education Research, 1(3), 22-29.

Cirillo, F. (2006). The Pomodoro Technique. Retrieved from https://francescocirillo.com/pages/pomodoro-technique

Clark, R. C. (2017). Building Expertise: Cognitive Methods for Training and Performance Improvement. John Wiley & Sons.

Clark, V. L., & Creswell, J. W. (2014). Understanding Research: A Consumer's Guide. Pearson Education, Inc.

Council of Graduate Schools. (2007). Graduate education: The backbone of American competitiveness and innovation. Council of Graduate Schools.

Covey, S. R. (2004). The 8th Habit: From Effectiveness to Greatness. Free Press.

Creswell, J. W. (2014). Research design: Qualitative, quantitative, and mixed methods approaches. SAGE Publications.

Creswell, J. W., & Creswell, J. D. (2017). Research Design: Qualitative, Quantitative, and Mixed Methods Approaches (5th ed.). Sage Publications.

Creswell, J. W., & Creswell, J. D. (2017). Research Design: Qualitative, Quantitative, and Mixed Methods Approaches. Sage Publications.

Creswell, J. W., & Creswell, J. D. (2017). Research design: Qualitative, quantitative, and mixed methods approaches (4th ed.). Sage Publications.

Creswell, J. W., & Creswell, J. D. (2017). Research design: Qualitative, quantitative, and mixed methods approaches. Sage publications.

Cronin, B. (2005). The Hand of Science: Academic Writing and Its Rewards. Scarecrow Press.

Davis, G. B., & Parker, C. A. (1997). Writing the Doctoral Dissertation: A Systematic Approach. Barron's Educational Series, Inc.

Dawson, C. (2019). Practical Research Methods. UPA.

Denzin, N. K. (1978). The Research Act: A Theoretical Introduction to Sociological Methods. McGraw-Hill.

DiCicco-Bloom, B., & Crabtree, B. F. (2006). The qualitative research interview. Medical Education, 40(4), 314-321.

Doe, J., Adams, R., & Thomas, H. (2021). Getting Published: The Academic's Guide to Smashing it Out of the Park. Journal of Academic Writing, 11(1), 54-72.

Doran, G. T. (1981). There's a S.M.A.R.T. way to write management's goals and objectives. Management Review, 70(11), 35-36.

Elbow, P. (1998). Writing without teachers (2nd ed.). New York, NY: Oxford University Press.

Endersby, J. W. (2012). Writing the Discussion section of a scientific paper. Scientific Communication and Education, 41(3), 241-245.

Etikan, I., Musa, S. A., & Alkassim, R. S. (2016). Comparison of convenience sampling and purposive sampling. American Journal of Theoretical and Applied Statistics, 5(1), 1-4.

Field, A. (2013). Discovering Statistics Using IBM SPSS Statistics. Sage.

Figueiredo, A.D. & Alarcão, I. (2007). Students' experiences of interdisciplinarity: towards a framework for evaluating higher education curriculum innovations. Teaching in Higher Education, 12(3), 349-363.

Fiorella, L., & Mayer, R. E. (2015). Learning as a generative activity: Eight learning strategies that promote understanding. Cambridge University Press.

Fisher, C. B. (2013). Decoding the Ethics Code: A Practical Guide for Psychologists. Sage Publications.

Flower, L., & Hayes, J. R. (1981). A cognitive process theory of writing. College Composition and Communication, 32(4), 365-387.

Franzosi, R. (2016). From words to numbers: Narrative, data, and social science. Cambridge University Press.

Fry, B. (2014). Visualizing Data. O'Reilly Media.

Gardner, S. K., Janssen, L. F., & Kumar, A. D. (2022). Finding work-life balance: Strategies for managing time in academia. Educational Researcher, 51(4), 246-259.

Golafshani, N. (2003). Understanding reliability and validity in qualitative research. The Qualitative Report, 8(4), 597-607.

Golde, C. M., & Walker, G. E. (2006). Envisioning the future of doctoral education: Preparing stewards of the discipline. Jossey-Bass.

Gopen, G. D., & Swan, J. A. (1990). The Science of Scientific Writing. American Scientist, 78(6), 550–558.

Guillot, M. (2012). The importance of an academic network. Journal of Scholarly Engagement, 1(1), 45-54.

Hamilton, J., & McMillan, V. (2021). Networking strategies for scholars and researchers. Higher Education Quarterly, 75(1), 97-110.

Harding, K. (2007). Choosing the right conference. Nature, 446, 240.

Harris, L. R., & Carter, M. (2019). The Reflective Doctoral Student: How to Absorb Critique While Maintaining Confidence. Higher Education Quarterly, 73(4), 394-407.

Hart, C. (1998). Doing a literature review: Releasing the social science research imagination. SAGE.

Hart, C. (2018). Doing a Literature Review: Releasing the Research Imagination. SAGE Publications.

Hartley, J. (2008). Academic writing and publishing: A practical handbook. Routledge.

Harzing, A.-W., & Alakangas, S. (2016). Google Scholar, Scopus and the Web of Science: A longitudinal and cross-disciplinary comparison. Scientometrics, 106(2), 787–804.

Hattie, J., & Timperley, H. (2007). The Power of Feedback. Review of Educational Research, 77(1), 81-112.

Hawkins, J. (2021). Academic Writing for Graduate Students: Essential Skills and Tasks. Michigan ELT.

Heale, R., & Twycross, A. (2015). Validity and reliability in quantitative studies. Evidence-Based Nursing, 18(3), 66-67.

Henshall, C. (2019). Managing and Organizing Your Collection of References for Your PhD: The Tool Kit Part I. Psychreg Journal of Psychology, 3(1), 8–14.

Herr, K., & Anderson, G. L. (2015). The Action Research Dissertation: A Guide for Students and Faculty. SAGE Publications.

Hyland, K. (2005). Metadiscourse: Exploring interaction in writing. Continuum.

Johnson, A., Smith, B., & Liu, C. (2022). Deviations in Conventional Understanding. Journal of Innovative Research, 48(3), 205-219.

Johnson, D. (2021). The Confident Speaker's Handbook: A Practical, Hands-On Approach to Public Speaking. Second Edition. SpeakEasy Publications.

Johnson, L., & Smith, J. (2017). Post-defense realities: Managing expectations and revisions in the dissertation process. Journal of Academic Persistence, 12(2), 34-45.

Kearns, H., Gardiner, M., & Marshall, K. (2016). Innovation in PhD completion: the hardy shall succeed (and be happy!). Postgraduate Medical Journal, 92(1084), 105-110.

Kehoe, J. L., Ku, H. Y., & O'Connell, A. A. (2019). The impact of the dissertation defense process on students' academic identity development. Journal of Higher Education Theory and Practice, 19(6), 19-33.

Kenney, J. (2020). Effective Strategies for Responding to Questions in an Academic Context. Postgraduate Student Journal, 5(1), 47-58.

Kumar, R. (2019). Research Methodology: A Step-by-Step Guide for Beginners. SAGE Publications Ltd.

Lillis, T. M., & Curry, M. J. (2010). Academic writing in a global context: The politics and practices of publishing in English. Routledge.

Locke, E. A., & Latham, G. P. (2002). Building a practically useful theory of goal setting and task motivation: A 35-year odyssey. American Psychologist, 57(9), 705-717.

Locke, L. F., Silverman, S. J., & Spirduso, W. W. (2009). Proposals that work: A guide for planning dissertations and grant proposals (6th ed.). Sage Publications.

Locke, L. F., Spirduso, W. W., & Silverman, S. J. (2020). Proposals that work: A guide for planning dissertations and grant proposals. SAGE Publications.

Maslach, C., & Leiter, M. P. (2016). Understanding the burnout experience: recent research and its implications for psychiatry. World Psychiatry, 15(2), 103-111.

Maxwell, J. A. (2012). Qualitative research design: An interactive approach (Vol. 41). Sage publications.

Maxwell, J. A. (2013). Qualitative research design: An interactive approach (Vol. 41). Sage publications.

Maxwell, J. A. (2020). Qualitative research design: An interactive approach (4th ed.). SAGE Publications, Inc.

Maxwell, J. C. (2017). Networking like a pro. Business Expert Press.

Mayer, R. E., & Moreno, R. (2003). Nine ways to reduce cognitive load in multimedia learning. Educational Psychologist, 38(1), 43-52.

McKinney, W. (2017). Python for Data Analysis: Data Wrangling with Pandas, NumPy, and IPython. O'Reilly Media.

Menard, S. (2002). Longitudinal Research. Sage Publications.

Merriam, S. B., & Tisdell, E. J. (2015). Qualitative research: A guide to design and implementation. Jossey-Bass.

Morse, J. M. (1991). Approaches to qualitative-quantitative methodological triangulation. Nursing Research, 40(2), 120-123.

Morse, J. M. (2016). Mixed method design: Principles and procedures. Routledge.

Mullins, G., & Kiley, M. (2002). It's a PhD, not a Nobel Prize": a model for examining the stress associated with the postgraduate experience. Higher Education Research & Development, 21(4), 41-54.

Mullins, G., & Kiley, M. (2002). 'It's a PhD, not a Nobel Prize': How experienced examiners assess research theses. Studies in Higher Education, 27(4), 369-386.

Murray, R. (2011). How to write a thesis. Open University Press.

Nicholas, D., & Watkinson, A. (2014). Publishing: A helping hand. Nature, 510(7504), 213-214.

No references are cited in this introduction.

Onwuegbuzie, A. J., & Frels, R. (2016). Seven steps to a comprehensive literature review: A multimodal and cultural approach. Sage.

Orwell, G. (1946). Politics and the English Language. Horizon, 13(76), 252–265.

Peng, R. D. (2011). Reproducible Research in Computational Science. Science, 334(6060), 1226-1227.

Phillips, E., & Pugh, D. S. (2015). How to get a Ph.D.: A handbook for students and their supervisors. New York, NY: McGraw-Hill Education.

Powers, J. T., Cook, J. E., Purdie-Vaughns, V., Garcia, J., Apfel, N., & Cohen, G. L. (2018). Changing environments by changing individuals: The emergent effects of psychological intervention. Psychological Science, 29(2), 230-239.

Prior, L. (2003). Using documents in social research. Sage Publications.

Pychyl, T. A., & Flett, G. L. (2012). Procrastination and self-regulatory failure: An introduction to the special issue. Journal of Rational-Emotive & Cognitive-Behavior Therapy, 30(4), 203-212.

Randolph, J. J. (2009). A guide to writing the dissertation literature review. Practical Assessment, Research & Evaluation, 14(13), 1-13.

Randolph, J. J. (2009). A guide to writing the dissertation literature review. Practical Assessment, Research, and Evaluation, 14(13), 1-13.

Ratey, J. J. (2008). Spark: The revolutionary new science of exercise and the brain. Little, Brown.

Repko, A. F. (2012). Interdisciplinary research: Process and theory. SAGE Publications.

Resnik, D. B. (2011). What is Ethics in Research & Why is it Important?. National Institute of Environmental Health Science.

Resnik, D. B. (2011). What is ethics in research & why is it important? National Institute of Environmental Health Sciences. Retrieved from https://www.niehs.nih.gov/research/resources/bioethics/whatis/index.cfm

Ridley, D. (2012). The Literature Review: A Step-by-Step Guide for Students (2nd ed.). Sage Publications.

Rocco, T. S., & Hatcher, T. (2011). The handbook of scholarly writing and publishing. Jossey-Bass.

Rowe, N. & Ilic, D. (2011). Poster Presentation – a visual medium for academic and scientific meetings. Paediatric Respiratory Reviews, 12(3), 208–213.

Rowley, J., & Slack, F. (2004). Conducting a literature review. Management Research News, 27(6), 31-39.

Roy Rosenzweig Center for History and New Media. (n.d.). Zotero | Your personal research assistant. Retrieved from https://www.zotero.org

Rudestam, K. E., & Newton, R. R. (2015). Surviving Your Dissertation: A Comprehensive Guide to Content and Process (4th ed.). SAGE Publications.

Schunk, D. H. (1991). Self-efficacy and academic motivation. Educational Psychologist, 26(3-4), 207-231.

Sheldon, K. M., & Lyubomirsky, S. (2006). How to increase and sustain positive emotion: The effects of expressing gratitude and visualizing best possible selves. The Journal of Positive Psychology, 1(2), 73-82.

Shuttleworth, M. (2008). Validity and reliability in quantitative studies. Explorable.

Silverman, D. (2017). Doing qualitative research (5th ed.). SAGE Publications Ltd.

Silvia, P. J. (2007). How to write a lot: A practical guide to productive academic writing. American Psychological Association.

Silvia, P. J. (2007). How to write a lot: A practical guide to productive academic writing. Washington, DC: American Psychological Association.

Silvia, P. J. (2014). How to Write a Lot: A Practical Guide to Productive Academic Writing. American Psychological Association.

Simons, H. (2015). Ethical Issues in Case Study Publication: "Making Our Case(s)" Ethically. Journal of Pediatric Health Care, 29(3), 221-223.

Smith, H. (2019). Strategies for building successful research networks. Academic Press.

Smith, J. A., & Davis, R. (2019). Understanding and addressing limitations in psychological research. Research in Psychology, 38(2), 215-220.

Smith, J. A., & Robertson, L. (2017). The Role of Continuing Education in Career Development. Adult Education Quarterly, 67(2), 128-145.

Smith, J., Fisher, G., & Walls, J. (2021). Developing and Proposing the Future Research Agenda. In The Handbook of Research Methods. Emerald Publishing Limited.

Smith, J., Flowers, P., & Larkin, M. (2019). Interpretative Phenomenological Analysis: Theory, Method, and Research. Sage Publications.

Smith, L., Fernandez, C., & Roberts, M. (2019). Building Confidence for Dummies. Wiley.

Snyder, C. (2021). The defense dilemma: Strategies for presenting qualitative research. Qualitative Report, 26(1), 120-130.

Stephan, P. E. (2012). How Economics Shapes Science. Harvard University Press.

Suddaby, R. (2014). Editor's comments: Why theory? Academy of Management Review, 39(4), 407-411.

Sue, V. M., & Ritter, L. A. (2012). Conducting Online Surveys. Sage Publications.

Sullivan, G. M., & Artino, A. R. Jr. (2013). Analyzing and interpreting data from Likert-type scales. Journal of Graduate Medical Education, 5(4), 541-542.

Swales, J. M., & Feak, C. B. (2012). Academic Writing for Graduate Students: Essential Tasks and Skills. University of Michigan Press.

Sword, H. (2012). Stylish academic writing. Harvard University Press.

Thomas, G. (2022). How to do your research project: A guide for students (4th ed.). SAGE Publications Ltd.

Thomas, R. J. (2021). Own your research: Understanding intellectual property in academia. Scholars' Rights Quarterly, 29(1), 50-64.

Thompson, C. J., & Kamler, B. (2013). Disconnects in the discussion section: New directions for research on the structure of scholarly papers in journals. Journal of Academic Writing, 23(1), 5-25.

Thompson, P. (2019). Peer Review and Manuscript Management in Scientific Journals: Guidelines for Good Practice. Wiley-Blackwell.

Thompson, S. K. (2012). Sampling (3rd ed.). Wiley.

Thomson, P., & Kamler, B. (2013). Writing for peer reviewed journals: Strategies for getting published. Routledge.

Tinkler, P., & Jackson, C. (2004). The Doctoral Examination Process: A Handbook For Students, Examiners And Supervisors. SRHE and Open University Press Imprint.

Tufte, E. R. (2001). The visual display of quantitative information (2nd ed.). Graphics Press.

University of Leicester. (2021). Preparing for your viva. University of Leicester. https://www2.le.ac.uk/offices/ld/resources/pgr/viva

University of North Carolina at Chapel Hill. (2022). Dissertation Defense Guidelines. UNC Graduate School. https://gradschool.unc.edu/academicguides/dissertations.html

Webster, J., & Watson, R. T. (2002). Analyzing the past to prepare for the future: Writing a literature review. MIS Quarterly, 26(2), xiii-xxiii.

Wellens, J., Malik, A., & Forsberg, L. (2021). Approaches to Preparing for Dissertation Defense: A Pedagogical Perspective. Journal of Graduate Education Research, 12(3), 203-215.

Wells, R. S. (2019). The Impact of Teaching on Academic Research. Science and Education, 28(3-5), 311-326.

Willis, G. B. (2016). Analysis of the cognitive interview in questionnaire design. Oxford University Press.

Wood, W., & Rünger, D. (2016). Psychology of Habit. Annual Review of Psychology, 67, 289-314.

Yin, R. K. (2013). Case Study Research: Design and Methods (5th ed.). Sage Publications.

Yin, R. K. (2018). Case study research and applications: Design and methods. Sage publications.

Zerubavel, E. (1999). The Clockwork Muse: A Practical Guide to Writing Theses, Dissertations, and Books. Harvard University Press.